TRUTH AND POLITICS

TRUTH AND POLITICS

Toward a Post-Secular Community

Fred Dallmayr

SUNY
PRESS

Cover image: Andrei Rublev, "Trinity."

Published by State University of New York Press, Albany

For information, contact State University of New York Press, Albany, NY
www.sunypress.edu

Library of Congress Cataloging-in-Publication Data

Name: Dallmayr, Fred, author.
Title: Truth and politics : toward a post-secular community / Fred Dallmayr, author.
Description: Albany : State University of New York Press, [2022] | Includes
    bibliographical references and index.
Identifiers: ISBN 9781438489698 (hardcover : alk. paper) | ISBN 9781438489711
    (ebook) | ISBN 9781438489704 (pbk. : alk. paper)
Further information is available at the Library of Congress.

10 9 8 7 6 5 4 3 2 1

Jesus called them together and said: "You know that the rulers of the Gentiles lord it over them and their great men exercise authority over them. It shall not be so among you, but whoever wants to be great among you, must be your servant."

—Matthew 20: 25–26; Mark 10: 42–43

The gospel of faith invites us to renew our spirit and to abandon destructive practices which separate us from each other, threatening the human family and the planet.

—Pope Francis

The evangelical impulse bears the imprint of a secularized Christianity and a sacred truth: that the energies of the gospel must pass into temporal life, that the good tidings throwing open heaven and eternal life also ask to transform earthly society in the midst of its woes and its contradictions.

—Jacques Maritain

When faithfulness is our standard, we are more likely to sustain our engagement with tasks that will never end: doing justice, loving mercy, and calling the beloved community into being.

—Richard Rohr

Democracy is a name for a life of free and enriching communion. It has its seer in Walt Whitman.

—John Dewey

CONTENTS

PREFACE

This book pursues a special purpose: it is meant to offer a therapy, a remedial help in troubled times. As we know, politics in recent times (especially in America) is in deep crisis. In many ways, political life is in turmoil, teetering on the edge of an abyss. In many quarters the view prevails that politics deals only with the struggle for power, with domination and manipulation and nothing else. This means that politics is entirely up for grabs, totally at the mercy of individual or partisan whims or interests—and thus completely devoid of any standard of truth.

This is the view that this book seeks to attack and demolish, because I hold it to be utterly wrong. There is, I maintain, a basic standard of truth in politics. It is neither an abstract-rational standard nor an arithmetic equation but a truth of human experience. I place myself here in the tradition of experiential political philosophy (from Aristotle to recent phenomenology and hermeneutics). What does this mean? It means that the truth I am talking about is not learned deductively but inductively through concrete practical life. This kind of induction is reserved not only for highly educated people and philosophers but is available to all people at all times regardless of age, gender, or particular culture.

The standard of truth I invoke is not arbitrary or optional but compelling because it is rooted in a basic existential reality: the distinction between life and death. Leaving aside minor nuances, there are historically two basic teachings about politics: one which is in the service of life and the other which is in the service of death. In the latter conception, politics means the struggle for power over others; more sharply formulated, politics means essentially the collision between "friend and enemy"—where the enemy is one who can be killed (and who retaliates by killing in turn). In the other conception, politics denotes the striving for the "good life," that is, a life marked by justice, equity, and equal respect for all. In ancient Rome, the Stoic philosophers, led by Cicero, used a catchy formula to express the gist of the life-affirming perspective: nonviolence and justice or fair treatment of all (*neminem laedere, suum cuique tribuere*). This standard had earlier been used by Greek philosophy (especially Aristotle) and was later endorsed by all great political thinkers East and West throughout history.

As mentioned before, this standard captures the "truth" of politics—not because it has been embraced by leading philosophers or written about in books, but because it is anchored in the core of human existence—which is located at the crossroads of life and death. It certainly captures my own existential experience. As a young boy, I was situated in Germany under the regime of Adolf Hitler. The "Führer" and his party firmly upheld the life-threatening conception that politics means the binary collision between friend and enemy. Implementing this conception, the regime sought to kill or exterminate all people who disagreed with its fascist (extreme-nationalist) creed. On this basis, Hitler involved all of Europe, and ultimately the entire world, in relentless warfare while simultaneously killing or exterminating all internal foes (culminating in the Holocaust). Following Hitler's downfall, Europe—under wise leadership—managed to return to the life-affirming conception of politics, a course which finally led to the creation of a united continent. This concrete experience—quite apart from mental cogitations and book learning—shaped my outlook for the rest of my life, helping me to heal the scars of my youth. Subsequently, for close to sixty years, I have taught the insight of the Stoic standard (nonviolence and justice) to students in many universities both at home and abroad.

Now, toward the end of my life (I am ninety-three), I find myself in a country in deep crisis. Many of the leading forces of the country, I notice, are attracted to the binary friend-enemy formula which had been the ruin of Europe not so long ago. To repeat, the formula encourages violence and killing, which leads to the destruction of others and ultimately to self-destruction. Thus, I feel the urgency to present or assemble some of my writings which uphold the nonbinary, life-enhancing perspective to the best of my abilities. Some of these essays or chapters have been published before, but at different locations which may be difficult to track down for ordinary readers. Here I have assembled them for easy access—just to show that I have not been silent or unresponsive to major social and political provocations. (The locations of some of the previously published chapters are listed in the acknowledgments.)

To add a point: the friend-enemy collision is just one of the binary conceptions which have troubled and are troubling our lives. There are other important binary views: the divorce between immanence and transcendence, between reason and faith, between secularism and post-secularism, between self and other (or nonself), between humanity and nature, and others. Actually, as I am indicating in some of the following chapters, the era of binary oppositions (which is largely the age of "modernity") seems to be coming to a close, opening up the prospect of a nontotalitarian connection or differential "relationality." This move to relationality is what is sometimes called a "paradigm shift," a shift which is quite crucial for a life-enhancing perspective and for the viable resurgence of the Stoic standard. The notion of a "truth" in or of politics should be seen in light of this paradigm shift. To this extent, the expression "truth and politics" bears a resemblance to Martin Heidegger's formulation of "Being and Time"—where "Being" (like truth) is always something distantly calling or challenging us, but waiting to be instantiated in time.

I want to tell students, readers, and all people of good will to change course: not to pursue passing passions; not to favor private or egocentric interests; not to subscribe to lies, fanciful ideas, or ideologies; but to be attentive to the truth of life and the truth of politics, which means to be mindful of the looming dangers of destruction and self-destruction. This, in turn, requires us to be fervently committed to life enhancement (in a nonegocentric way) and to the goal of justice, nonviolence, and peace.

To be sure, the notion of a "paradigm shift" seems to suggest a purely cognitive or academic exercise, which is completely misleading. Actually, this is one of the most difficult tasks human beings face: the struggle to move beyond self-interest and also beyond group or sectarian identity.

Thus, I do not ignore the personal and communal hardship which sometimes involves lostness and suffering. I do not ignore the profound words of Matthew (16:25–26): "Anyone who wants to save his/her life, must lose it; anyone who loses his/her life will find it." Obviously, this is a major challenge, one almost beyond human ability. But this shift which I delineate in these pages may actually have a chance to succeed—if we open our minds and ears and learn from difficult recent experiences. In this sense, I applaud Father Richard Rohr, who writes in *The Divine Dance*: The change "cannot come a moment too soon. Because I am convinced that beneath the ugly manifestation of our present evils—political corruption, ecological devastation, warring against one another, hating each other based on race, gender, religion, or sexual orientation—the greatest disease facing humanity right now is our profound and painful sense of disconnection."

In conclusion, the usual acknowledgments and expressions of gratitude are in order. As in the past, my thinking has been greatly stimulated and enriched by a number of colleagues and friends. Among them I want to mention this time especially Charles Taylor, Raimon Panikkar, William Connolly, Ruth Abbey, Marietta Stepaniants, Edward Demenchonok, Marie-Luisa Frick, and Richard Falk. I owe special thanks again to Cheryl Reed, who, with her usual competence and efficiency, has typed and helped correct several versions of this book (a task made particularly difficult by my advancing macular degeneration). As always, my deepest debt of gratitude goes to my family: my wife Ilse, our children Dominque and Philip, and our grandchildren. Their support carried me through the most difficult period of my life and of my adopted country, the winter of 2020–2021.

—Fred Dallmayr
October 2021

ACKNOWLEDGMENTS

Some of the material of this book has been previously published in different forms. I have drawn (with revisions) from the following sources:

"Post-Secularity and Global Politics: A Need for Redefinition," in my *Being and the World: Dialogue and Cosmopolis* (Lexington: University Press of Kentucky, 2013), 137–150.

"Post-Secular Faith: Toward a Religion of Service," in my *Integral Pluralism: Beyond Culture Wars* (Lexington: University Press of Kentucky, 2010), 67–84.

"A Secular Age? Reflections on Taylor and Panikkar," *International Journal of Philosophy of Religion* 71 (2012): 59–76.

"Man against the State: Self-Interest and Civil Resistance," *Social Imaginaries* 1 (2015): 1–24; also strongly revised from my *Freedom and Solidarity: Toward New Beginnings* (Lexington: University Press of Kentucky, 2016), 115–135.

"Neo-Liberalism and Its Critics: Voices from East and West," *Journal of the Indian Council for Philosophical Research* 24 (2008): 132–159.

"Individualized Life: The Plight or Narcissism," revised version of "Beyond Autistic Politics: Narcissism and Public Agency," *Philosophy and Social Criticism* 43 (2017): 989–999.

"Holism and Particularism: Panikkar on Human Rights," in *Raimundo Panikkar: A Pilgrim across Worlds*, ed. Kapila Vatsyayan and Côme Carpentier de Gourdin (New Delhi: Niyogi Books, 2016), 168–179.

1

INTRODUCTION

Emerging from Multiple Rifts

Our time is beset by numerous problems, dilemmas, and upheavals. Some of these dilemmas are routine and the normal feature of social life in every historical period. However, other dilemmas go deeper and affect the basic structure of social existence; in that case, one speaks of paradigmatic changes or "paradigm shifts." Our period is an epoch marked profoundly by such shifts. An age of deep changes necessarily is accompanied by intense agonies and traumatic experiences, but the same traumas also stir up fresh hopes and unregimented expectations. People wedded to the past are likely to deplore ongoing changes as a basic threat to their familiar way of life (and even to human life as such). On the other hand, people disillusioned with past arrangements are likely to embrace the future, despite the risks of untested adventures.[1]

The present book explores three kinds of paradigm shifts—or rather three dimensions of one overarching shift. The overarching shift is from separation or division to mutuality and correlation. Couched in broad historical terms (neglecting subtle details), the basic change is from "modernity" to an age which is usually called "post-modernity" or "post-modernism." By common consent, the "modern" period signaled a break from the preceding medieval age marked by holistic unity or uniformity. What was initiated by modernity is a dualistic rupture or division along several axes. One such axis is the division between the "sacred" and the "secular"—a rupture which is also expressed as the antinomy between "transcendence" and "immanence" or else between religious faith and human reason. Compared with this

1

vertical kind of division, another axis is located on a more horizontal level: the division between the "self" and the "other"—which also finds expression in the gulf between "self-interest" and community, between the "private" and the "public" domains (and also between ethnocentric nationalism and cross-cultural globalism). A third kind of rift has a more ontological character and involves the relation or nonrelation between nature and humanity or human designs. While at the height of modernity nature was entirely subject to human control, the paradigm change brings into view the prospect of closer collaboration and symbiosis. As one can see, the overall shift has a triadic character, corresponding to the triadic nature of reality or real-life experience.

The outcome of the contemporary paradigm shift is not the endorsement of one or the other side of the modern division, but rather the prospect of genuine mutuality or correlation—despite the recognition of a limited otherness or "difference."[2] Thus, with regard to the first axis mentioned before, we encounter the correction of the modern accent on worldly secularity—an accent accompanied by a limited role of religious faith in private life. In this correction, secularity or the importance of secular life is not abandoned, but rather transformed. The term commonly used for this transformed perspective is "post-secularity," or "post-secular faith." What happens in this new dispensation is that faith becomes relevant again for social and political life—but not in the mode of domination or mastery. Although rejecting the role of an ideological prop, faith in this new mode joins secular or worldly democracy whose ideal of the "good life" it shares. In traditional terminology, post-secular faith can be seen to hover at the cusp or boundary of immanence and transcendence. While transgressing purely worldly strategies or power plays, it simultaneously supports the secular struggle for democracy, equality, and peace, thus combining world and spirit.[3]

One of the chief proponents of post-secularity was the French religious philosopher Jacques Maritain, well known for his defense of an "integral humanism" located on the other side of a restrictive selfhood. As he wrote already in 1936: "It seems that the dualism of the preceding [modern] age is at an end. For the Christian, separation and dualism have had their day, because an important process of integration is taking place in our time, . . . a return to a vital synthesis."[4] In the present book, the first three chapters are devoted to the discussion of a number of other proponents of the idea, including Charles Taylor, Jürgen Habermas, Paul Ricoeur, William Connelly, and myself. In the third chapter I uphold an important change in the meaning of religion: the change from mental cognition to praxis, from the celebration of dogmas or dogmatic beliefs to the practical enactment of a "religion of service." I embrace at this point a statement written by Ricoeur half a century ago: "After several centuries during which Christians had been preoccupied chiefly with inner life and personal salvation, we are discovering afresh what is meant by 'you are the salt of the earth' (Matthew 5:13). We are discovering that the salt is made for salting, the light for illuminating, and that the church exists for the sake of those outside itself." In Ricoeur's view, Christ (and any religious figure) cannot or should not be invoked as an imperial potentate but only as a source of inspiration able "to give light once more to all people," that is, no longer "as a power, but as a prophetic message."[5]

With these words, a new "post-secular" correlation of faith and democracy was inaugurated, in a way which deserves the widest possible attention. Unfortunately, such attention is too often lacking today, being overshadowed or pushed aside by doctrines of religious mastery or imperialism. Examples of this backward-looking tendency can be found in many seemingly progressive countries, including the United States. A notorious example emerged in Germany during the past century when the so-called "German Christians" supported the policies of Adolf Hitler for "religious" reasons. In the words of Reverend Guthrie (speaking for "Faithful America"): "These appalling actions may have been taken in Jesus's name, but they do not speak for him. As Christians and other people of genuine faith, we are called to stand for justice, dignity and the common good—which means not putting up with arrogant and ultimately deadly leadership."[6]

Similar sentiments can be found in some of my own writings—as recorded for instance in chapter 4 of the present book. The chapter refers specifically to the cross-cultural religious thinker Raimon Panikkar. In his book *The Rhythm of Being*, Panikkar shows himself troubled by the conception of monotheistic "transcendence," because it agrees too readily with political despotism. As he writes: "The titles of King and Lord fit the monotheistic God quite well, and conversely, the human king could easily be the representative of God, and his retinue a copy of the heavenly hierarchies." In lieu of traditional transcendence, Panikkar boldly champions a radical relationality where "everything is permeated by everything else." Together with critiquing traditional monotheism his work also endorses a new trinitarian conception whose constituent elements (the Divine, humanity, and the natural world) interact with each other in a transformative rhythm or embrace: "Man is 'more' than just an individual being, the Divine different from a supreme Lord, and 'world' other than raw material to be plundered for utility or profit."[7] Views similar to these can also be found in my own *Small Wonder*, a text written roughly at the same time. Attentive to the arguments of both Panikkar and the Indian novelist Arundhati Roy, that text stated:

> For too long in human history the divine has been nailed to the cross of worldly power. However, in recent times, there are signs that the old alliance may be ending and that religious faith may begin to liberate itself from the chains of worldly manipulation. Exiting from the palaces and mansions of the powerful, faith—joined by philosophers' wisdom—is beginning to take shelter in inconspicuous smallness, in the recession of ordinary life unavailable to co-optation.[8]

These comments clearly point to the second dimension of the ongoing paradigm shift: the relation between "self" and "other," differently stated, between individual self-interest and community concerns or between "private" and "public" domains of life. In this respect, modernity has introduced a sharp division by accentuating the pursuit of self-interest, and by elevating the more powerful or selfish individuals as rulers over the multitude. This divisive tendency has been gaining momentum during the past two centuries, and today has reached its zenith (at least in the West). A good analysis is provided by Jean Bethke Elshtain in her book *Democracy on Trial* (1995) which, focusing mainly on American democracy, pinpoints as its central concern "the danger of losing democratic civil society" under the onslaught of rampant fragmentation and self-aggrandizement. In Elshtain's view, although a properly construed democracy is not "boundlessly subjectivist" or individualistic, the worry is that "it has, over time, become so." Once this happens, the spirit of democracy—especially the love of equality—vanishes, making room instead for "other more fearful and self-enclosed, more suspicious and cynical habits and dispositions."[9] What her book clearly anticipated was the rise of (what is called) "neo-liberalism" and "laissez-faire" politics, whose result is the inevitable undercutting of democracy as a shared political regime. Similar views have been expressed by the philosopher Ronald Dworkin in a text titled *Is Democracy Possible Here?* (2006), a question which he answered at best ambivalently. In his words: "American politics is in an appalling state. We are no longer partners in [democratic] self-government; our politics are rather a form of war."[10]

The present study devotes three chapters to the progressive decline of modern politics into neo-liberalism or divisive "libertarianism." In this decline individual ambition is progressively glorified, while the public realm of the "state" or community is reduced to a machine controlled by experts. As chapter 5 shows, this development can be found in "utilitarianism," which located the engine of human conduct in the "pleasure and pain" calculus, and also in biological evolutionism or "Social Darwinism" with its stress on physical ability or power. An early culmination of these trends was reached in the work of Herbert Spencer, especially his book *The Man versus the State* (1884), where the "state" was largely identified with a big bureaucratic structure, while "man" was equated with a presocial individual. In Spencer's words: "There are no phenomena which a society presents but that have their origin in the phenomena of individual life, which again have their roots in vital [natural] phenomena at large."[11] The character of the relation between individual and the "state" for Spencer was basically a nonrelation ("versus") which could not be bridged because of the technical apparatus of the state. What this dualist view neglected is the possible cultivation of shared concerns in the midst of social conflict, that is, the possibility of "civil disobedience" as resistance to or critique of perceived public abuses. Whereas, in Spencer's case, anti-public conduct was rooted in sheer self-interest, the point of genuine civil disobedience is precisely to restore public well-being and justice. To illustrate the character of the second possibility I turn to Henry David Thoreau, a contemporary of Spencer, and later to Albert Camus and Dietrich Bonhoeffer (in the context of Nazi Germany).

The lure of neo-liberalism has not come to an end. Under such labels as "rational choice theory" or "minimal democracy," the neo-liberal agenda has been promoted by a number of prominent American intellectuals. Chapter 6 in this study draws attention to such scholars as Robert Dahl, Giovanni Sartori, and William Riker, scholars concerned mainly with the compatibility of a "minimal democracy" with capitalist economics. In Riker's words: "No government that has eliminated economic freedom has been able to attain or keep democracy"; seen in this light, "economic liberty is an end in itself because capitalism is the driving force."[12] Chapter 6 contrasts this outlook with the tradition of "Jacksonian democracy" and, more importantly, with John Dewey's defense of "radical" democracy as an antidote to minimalist or "laissez-faire" democracy. As one of his students has pointed out: For Dewey "democracy as an ideal for community life is not a mere provision for a minimal state which simply leaves citizens alone. Such an individualistic ideal is inimical to the kind of *associated* [correlated] living which is democratic."[13]

The chapter also draws attention to some global or cross-cultural voices critical of American minimalism. In the South Asian contexts the main voice is that of Mahatma Gandhi as expressed in his *Hind Swaraj* (*Indian Home Rule*) of 1909. For Gandhi, home rule or self-rule (*swaraj*) does not mean selfish rule or the promotion of private ambitions, but rather the ability to channel such ambitions in the direction of the common or societal good. As he wrote in *Hind Swaraj*: "Civilization is that mode of conduct which points out to human beings the path of duty (*dharma*). Performance of ethical duty means to attain mastery over our mind and our passions." The clear implication of this view is a new understanding of democracy: not as the pursuit of individual or collective self-interest but in the service of a transformative public self-rule.[14] In the East Asian context, the main antipode to minimalism is Confucianism as interpreted chiefly by Tu Weiming. For the Chinese thinker, Confucianism opposes both negative and positive liberty, that is, the construal of freedom in terms of either private withdrawal from society or public domination. In his words: it rejects both the affirmation of the self as "an isolable, complacent ego" and its total immersion in the world for the sake of "manipulative power." In lieu of these alternatives, the Confucian "way" (*tao*) demands an "unceasing process of self-transformation as a communal act."[15]

The culmination of the modern stress on antisocial selfishness can be seen in the rise of what one may call "autistic politics," that is, the ascent of self-love or narcissism to a form of public conduct. Chapter 7 discusses this novel blending of psychoanalysis and public discourse. Already in 1979, Christopher Lasch had sounded the alarm by claiming that, in our time, narcissism is no longer just a private ailment but has gained the status of a social pathology and even a "public culture."[16] The chapter discusses first of all the portrayal of this startling phenomenon by Zygmunt Bauman. As he writes in *Liquid Modernity* (2000): "The whole of modernity stands out from preceding epochs by its compulsive and obsessive modernizing—and modernizing means liquefaction," which in turns means disengagement and dissolution. The chief accent of modernity, he notes, is on private freedom, which clashes with civic obligations to the point that the individual becomes "the citizen's worst enemy."[17] In *The Individualized Society* (2001) Bauman— following Lasch—speaks of a "culture" of egotism and disengagement, a condition which has as a corollary the breakdown of civic solidarity.[18]

Adopting a cross-cultural perspective, the chapter turns to the prominent Indian psychologist Ashis Nandy, especially his study *Regimes of Narcissism, Regimes of Despair* (2013). In Nandy's view, a "clenched-teeth pursuit of happiness" has become a major feature of our time—but a feature which boomerangs, yielding instead the rise of death wishes, suicide epidemics, and psychic disorders.[19] In recent times, social atomism has been intensified worldwide by the spreading of the pandemic (COVID-19) and its corollaries of face masking and social distancing. To find a counterweight to disaggregation I lift up the work of Hannah Arendt, whose writings bridge the gulf between ego and society by celebrating the notions of "common sense," shared world experience, and the cultivation of public civility.

The present study does not concentrate on the third dimension of the paradigm shift of our time: the relation or nonrelation between "man" and nature. As we know, an aspect of this dimension has lately thrust itself into the foreground of life, everywhere, under the impact of the pandemic, of coronavirus. Although not specifically dwelling on man-nature issues here, I definitely consider its role as paradigmatic, as it calls for a reformulation of constitutive elements (away from exploitation to symbiosis). On other occasions I have commented on this crucial dimension, paying attention—apart from horrible diseases—to aspects of climate change and ecological mutations.[20] I am particularly fond of a statement by Thomas Berry, a Passionate Priest, to the effect that "there is no such thing as a 'human community' without the earth and the soil and the air and the water and all the living forms. Without these, humans do not exist. Humans are woven into this larger community which is a sacred community."[21]

In the present context I prefer to return to the broad picture of paradigm shift. The words of Berry would certainly have been applauded by his fellow priest, the eco-sophist and post-modern nondualist Raimon Panikkar. Chapter 8 focuses on a central issue of modernity: the stress on human freedom which finds expression in the notion of "human rights." Together with other "post-secularists" Panikkar fully accepts the importance of rights as a cornerstone of modern social and political life. But the basic question for him concerns a communal and holistic background: Do rights necessarily have to be construed in a dualistic or antagonistic sense, where the rights of some individuals or groups inevitably trump or negate the rights of others? He finds a possible solution or remedy in the Indian notion of *dharma* as recorded in the Dharmashastras, the *Bhagavad Gita*, and the great epics.

As he notes in a pertinent text, the term *dharma* is perhaps "the most fundamental word" in the entire Indian tradition, a term seeking to provide "cohesion and thus strength to any given thing" and ultimately to the "three worlds" (*triloka*) of the cosmos. Yet given his post-modern perspective, Panikkar—bypassing an extreme holism or collectivism—recognizes the difference of rights in particular circumstances and perspectives. This means that the difference between claims and counterclaims, between rights and duties, has to be carefully negotiated in a civil manner; above all the pursuit of particular rights has to be tallied with civic responsibilities, especially the task of world-maintenance (*lokasamgraha*). Thus, what for Panikkar is needed is the "mutual fecundation" of cultures and discourses, above all a "diatopial dialogue" involving the movement between different contexts or places (*topoi*).[22]

The Catalan Indian priest passed away in 2010, thus being spared the experience of recent secular turmoil and rifts. His legacy, however, is profound and far-reaching.[23] Some of the main thrusts of his work have been continued by the Franciscan priest Richard Rohr, whose work is the topic of chapter 9. Rohr is the founding director of the Center for Action and Contemplation in Albuquerque, whose name already signals its "post-secular" aim: namely, the combination of worldly/secular engagement with reflection on the spiritual/religious roots of engaged life. The same balance is evident in Rohr's endorsement of freedom and human rights, which is coupled with his simultaneous stress on nonaggressive or nondualist symbiosis. The closest affinity with Panikkar emerges in his conception of religion or religious faith—where faith is not or no longer tied to an imperial "monotheism" but manifests itself in the practice of mutual love and solidarity.

Importantly, this nonimperial faith is not limited to a particular church or doctrine but has a universal or cross-cultural significance (deriving from the universality of "Christ" as divine source of all beings).[24] Together with the Catalan Indian, Rohr also champions a new kind of trinitarianism whose components are not fixed or static entities but rather partners in a rhythmic or dancelike process of ongoing revelation and transformation.[25] One of the most important and innovative contributions of the Franciscan is his correlation of downfall or transgression with the promise of spiritual rescue or uplift. As a student of St. Bonaventure, he endorses the "coincidence of opposites," thus arguing that human lapse or fall into darkness can trigger a divinely ordained "falling upward" toward the light—which can also have a communal and political significance.[26] The concluding remarks shift attention to the recent secular turmoil manifest in attacks on public civility and democratic equality. As a timely remedy or antidote, I invoke the work of Martin Luther King Jr., especially his book pitting contemporary chaos against the promise of a spiritual democratic community.[27] At this point, I also recall the poem "The Hill We Climb" by Amanda Gorman, the "inaugural poet," uplifting the hopeful promise of a new civility and the prospect of a Great Community among people in the world.

2

POST-SECULARITY
AND (GLOBAL) POLITICS

A Need for Redefinition

I will put my law within them, and I will write it upon their hearts.

—Jeremiah 31:33

In recent intellectual discussions, the term "post-secularity" has acquired a
certain currency or prominence. Like other hyphenated terms (post-modernism, post-metaphysics), the word exudes a certain irenic quality, in the
sense that the harsh features of traditional conflicts—between faith and reason, religion and agnosticism—are presumably mitigated if not laid to rest.
Unfortunately, this hope may be mistaken. Like many similar labels, the term
"post-secularity" papers over disputes of interpretation which cannot simply
be brushed aside. For some interpreters—clinging to the prefix "post"—the
term signals the end of a loathed or despised aspect of modernity, its lapse
into irreligion and agnostic "secularism," thus heralding a return to old-style
religious orthodoxy (possibly under clerical auspices). Seen from this angle,
the hyphenated expression means the correction of an errancy, an outgrowth
of what Gilles Kepel has called "the revenge of God."[1] For another type of
interpreter—attached to secularity or secularism—the phrase is a conces-
sion to the Zeitgeist, to the inevitably multicultural and multidimensional
character of contemporary democracy. Averse to dogmatism and stirred by
their "liberal" conscience, secular agnostics are willing to accommodate or

9

tolerate deviant nonconformists including religious people—provided their conduct and utterances submit to the dominant language game.

Thus, underneath the seemingly irenic phrase, the older animosities and resentments still persist; behind the façade of a hyphenated term, traditional culture wars continue. In some fashion, for both sides of the dispute, the terms "secularism" and "secularity" designate a "worldly" domain basically immune from "otherworldly" intrusion, a realm of "immanence" categorically opposed to religious "transcendence." The two sides differ in placing their evaluative preference respectively in opposing domains; the hyphenated phrase reflects mainly a pragmatic compromise. The question remains, however, whether the stipulated dichotomy—often styled "two-world" theory—can really be maintained.

At a closer look, the dichotomy is quickly thrown into disarray. On a purely logical level, the two terms—immanence and transcendence—presuppose each other as mutual conditions of possibility—which means that they cannot be radically separated. More importantly, simple etymology contests such separation. Deriving from the Latin *saeculum* (age/century), secularism basically refers to the necessary time dimension of human experience—a temporality which inevitably permeates both reason and faith, both "worldly" cognition and religion (thus undercutting their presumed contrast). In the following I want to pursue these issues further. In a first step, I review the persisting conflict within "post-secularity," that is, the conflict between post-secular "secularists" and post-secular (or post-modern) religious traditionalists. What this review yields, I believe, is a basic commonality: namely, the shared and inevitable reliance on interpretation or hermeneutics—a point developed in a second step. By way of conclusion, I want to indicate the genuine relevance of "post-secularity"—properly interpreted—for both domestic democracy and the emerging global cosmopolis.

Secularity versus Faith

In mainstream liberal-democratic theory, the political regime is supposed to be removed from, and hence basically neutral toward, religion(s) or what are called "comprehensive worldviews." This conception was formulated most famously in the early writings of philosopher John Rawls. In subsequent years, however, this formula of sequestering religion in a private faith, removed from the public domain, was found to be too rigid and also not quite compatible with democratic standards (mandating the "free exercise of religion"). Hence, religion was allowed—within limits—to reenter the public realm, provided certain conditions regarding public conduct and linguistic discourse were met.[2] It is at this point that Jürgen Habermas—one of the originators of the term "post-secularity"—joins the debate.

In several writings published during the past decades, Habermas has sought to pinpoint clearly the conditions under which religion might reenter the public sphere. Thus, in an essay published in 2008 on "An Awareness of What Is Missing," Habermas stressed the stark distance separating modern enlightened reason from religious faith, a distance which also reflects stages of historical development. "The philosophically enlightened self-understanding of modernity," we read, "stands in a peculiar dialectical [conflictual?] relationship to the theological self-understanding of the major world religions which intrude into this modernity as the most awkward element from its past." From the angle of modern reason, both religion and traditional metaphysical worldviews have an ambivalent status: they are rejected in their present validity though (grudgingly) accepted as historical precursors. While acknowledging metaphysics "as belonging to the prehistory of its own emergence," modern thought "treats revelation and religion as something alien and extraneous." As Habermas insists, "the cleavage between secular knowledge and revealed knowledge cannot be bridged"—although secular or "post-metaphysical" reason may concede "the shared origin of philosophy and religion in the revolution of the Axial Age."[3]

In his essay, Habermas clearly accepts the Rawlsian formula regarding the relation between the public and private domains. "The constitutional state," he writes, "must not only act neutrally towards worldviews but it must rest on normative foundations which can be justified neutrally towards worldviews—and that means in post-metaphysical [i.e., secular] terms." This formula clearly imposes a heavy and primary burden on faith. "The religious communities," he adds, "cannot turn a deaf ear to this normative requirement." In fact, "the content of religion must open itself up to the normatively grounded expectation that it should recognize, for reasons of its own, the neutrality of the state towards worldviews. . . . This is a momentous step." Following the more "liberal" or accommodating arguments of the later Rawls, however, the essay also seeks to ease the burden imposed on religious belief: "Conversely, the secular state . . . must also face the question of whether it is imposing asymmetrical obligations on its religious citizens. For the liberal state guarantees the equal freedom to exercise religion not only as a means of upholding law and order, but also for the normative reason of protecting the freedom of belief and conscience of everyone." The upshot of this argument is the compromise that the state "may not demand anything of its religious citizens which cannot be reconciled with a life that is led authentically 'from faith.'" What is presupposed in this compromise, however, is the availability and maintenance of a common language in the public field, and this requisite brings into the foreground the issue of translation.[4]

From a secular or post-secular vantage point (that of Habermas), the situation is not only that the "cleavage" between secular reason and revelation "cannot be bridged," but that there are two different languages or discourses whose sharp contrast cannot be overcome except through an effort of translation—an effort designed to render religious idioms publicly available. The assumption here is that there is a standard public discourse whose language is readily accessible, while religious language is odd, obsolete, and esoteric—although secular citizens are exhorted "not to treat religious expressions as simply irrational" (which is a widespread temptation). If modern liberal democracy is to function, Habermas affirms, a common language is required, and for this requisite to be secured, "two presuppositions" must be fulfilled:

> The religious side must accept the authority of "natural" reason
> as the fallible result of the institutionalized sciences and the basic
> principles of universalistic egalitarianism in law and morality.
> Conversely, secular reason may not set itself up as the judge
> concerning the "truths" of faith—even though in the end it can
> accept as reasonable only what it can translate into its own, in
> principle universally accessible, discourses.

What this means is that modern secular discourses are self-contained and wholly accessible or intelligible on their own terms, without the need of translation or interpretation—whereas the very opposite is the case for religious language. The self-containment of secular reason even seems to shield it against philosophical or interpretive questioning. Modern science, Habermas asserts, enables modern rationality to break with all "metaphysical" issues: "With this advance in reflection, nature and history became the preserve of the empirical sciences, and not much more is left for philosophy than the general competence of knowing, speaking, and acting subjects."[5]

About a year later, at a conference held in New York, Habermas reiterated and fleshed out further his views on the role of religion in the "public sphere." After touching on a number of issues (including Carl Schmitt's notion of "the political"), he returned there to the Rawlsian formula mentioned before and its limitations. As he pointed out, Rawls's formula had met the critique that "many citizens *cannot* or *are not willing* to make the required separation between contributions expressed in religious terms and those expressed in secular language." Moreover, the formula suffers from a democratic deficit given that a liberal regime "also exists to safeguard religious forms of life" and hence cannot excise religious language. It is at this point that the translation proposal recurs. "According to this proposal," Habermas states, "all citizens should be free to decide whether they want to use religious language in the public sphere"—with the crucial proviso that "were they to do so, they would have to accept that the potential truth contents of religious utterances must be translated into a generally accessible language before they can find their way into the agendas of parliaments, courts, or administrative bodies." Fine-tuning his proposal, Habermas introduces the further distinction between formal and informal language, a distinction monitored by a screening filter: instead of requiring citizens to cleanse their comments of religious rhetoric, "an institutional filter should be established between informal communication in the public arena and formal deliberations of political bodies that lead to collectively binding decisions." In this manner, a "universally accessible language" is secured in the public sphere, while "the 'monolingual' contributions of religious citizens depend on the translational efforts of cooperative fellow citizens (if they are not to fall on deaf ears)."[6]

The emphasis on translation efforts and complex filtering devices attests to the presumed distance between religion and modern rationality—what Habermas earlier had called the unbridgeable "cleavage between secular knowledge and revealed knowledge." What this means is that religious people and secular rationalists are divided not only by different beliefs but by a linguistic gulf which is as deep as (and maybe even deeper than) the gulf between English and Chinese. Presumably, adepts of religion are proficient in some kind of "metaphysical" or "otherworldly" language, whereas secularists are fluent in vernacular or "this-worldly" language. Clearly, what surfaces here in new guise is the old "two-world" theory, now couched in linguistic vocabulary. Together with that theory, we also encounter again the ancient conundrum which has variously been termed the rift between "Athens and Jerusalem" or (more simply) between knowledge and faith. Curiously, in our contemporary period, the rift is affirmed not only by secularists—including those favoring translation devices—but also by radical religious thinkers thoroughly opposed to secularism and modernity. In the latter case, the "post" in post-secularity acquires a very different meaning: namely, that of a farewell or demise.

Insisting on the stark distance between "this" world and the next, an assumption has recently emerged in various quarters which extols the radical "otherness," transcendence, and unintelligibility of the sacred or divine—thereby reviving the famous dictum of Tertullian: "What has Jerusalem got to do with Athens?"[7] Once the division is construed as cleavage, the sacred or divine can enter the "worldly" domain—including the domain of human understanding—only by way of irruption, interruption, or disruption—which amounts to a form of violence or violation. My concern here is not with the different ways in which this conception is expressed in our time. On a popular level, we are only too familiar with such modes of religious extravagance as the celebration of "rapture" and the speedy arrival of Armageddon. On a more recessed and sober level, traces of exuberance can also be found among some "post-modern" thinkers, especially supporters of a "transcendentalist" phenomenology and a radical type of post- or anti-hermeneutics. Despite differences of accent, what is common to these tendencies is the stress on divine incommensurability, on the nonreciprocity or nonrelational character of the sacred and secular realms. Occasionally, sacred intervention is styled as a divine largesse or "gift"—but with no ability granted to recipients to recognize divine largesse "as" a gift. Carried to an extreme and transferred to a linguistic register, the separation of worlds implies not only a difference of language games but their actual nontranslatability. On this and similar issues I find it preferable to follow Italian philosopher Gianni Vattimo, who counsels us to be "suspicious of an excessive emphasis on the transcendence of God, as mystery, radical alterity, and paradox" and to return to the simplicity of the gospels.[8]

Religion and Ordinary Language

Vattimo's counsel, to be sure, applies not only to exuberant post-modernists but also—with equal force—to secular "post-secularists" championing the integrity of modern rational discourse. As presented by Habermas, modern discourse—as used by rationalist thinkers as well as by legal courts and parliaments—is claimed to be readily and universally accessible, whereas religious discourse is the opposite: mysterious and urgently in need of translation. But how persuasive is this argument? Are modern rationalist texts—from Kant to Carnap, Quine, and Rawls—not exceedingly difficult texts constantly in need of interpretation and reinterpretation, and hence of translation into more accessible language? And what about courts?

Do the judgments of courts not always involve the interpretation, application, and thus practical translation of earlier legal texts, precedents, and judicial opinions? And do members of parliament not always claim to interpret, apply, and hence translate the will of the "people" (or at least of their constituents)? And where is there an end to such interpretation and translation, that is, the effort to distill the meaning of texts, utterances, and events and thus to render them accessible to understanding? As recent "post-empiricist" epistemology attests, the range of interpretation extends even to scientific paradigms and the findings of natural science. As it seems to me, these comments only confirm the truth kernel of the hermeneutical claim of "universality"—a claim prominently articulated by Hans-Georg Gadamer (but sidestepped or neglected by Habermas).[9] No doubt, the demand for interpretation also applies to religious teachings; but as I shall try to show, the demand here may be less urgent and involve not so much a strictly linguistic translation but a translation into lived practice.

The one-sided or lopsided character of the Habermasian translation proviso has been noted by several observers but especially by Charles Taylor. In his 2009 response to the former titled "Why We Need a Radical Redefinition of Secularism," Taylor takes issue with the assumption shared by Rawls and Habermas that modern secular reason is "a language that everyone speaks and can argue and be convinced in," whereas religious languages "operate outside this discourse by introducing extraneous premises that only believers can accept." In the case of Habermas, this distinction amounts not just to a linguistic difference but an "epistemic break" between secular reason and religious thought, "with the advantage on the side of the first."

In a somewhat provocative vein, Taylor speaks here of "a myth of the Enlightenment" where the legitimate demand for the use of reason is transformed into a shibboleth and shielded against any intrusions or trans-formative horizons. In the same context, Taylor links this shibboleth with the "principle of self-sufficient [or self-contained] reason" (which, in turn, seems to be connected with what he elsewhere calls the "buffering of the self" in modernity). For all their differences, he adds, Rawls and Habermas "seem to reserve a special status for non-religiously informed reason (let's call it 'reason alone')," assuming that such reason is able to resolve moral-political issues in a way "that can legitimately satisfy any honest, non-confused thinker"; by contrast, both find it necessary to "restrict the use of religious language in the sphere of public reason" by circumscribing this use with various translation and filtering devices. Summing up his discussion of this issue, Taylor concludes: "This distinction in rational credibility between religious and non-religious discourse seems to me utterly without foundation"—or else to rest on a rationalist "foundationalism" (stemming from Descartes) which is no longer credible.[10]

At this point, I want to push Taylor's argument a bit further by calling into question the notion of an "epistemic break" between modern secular reason and religious faith. In Habermas's account, both modern reason and religious faith seem to have the character of an epistemic or cognitive paradigm, each equipped with a *magisterium* designed to guard the integrity or correctness of the respective discourse. But this assumption seems to be implausible and the result of a misplaced "intellectualism." As it appears to me, at least the so-called Abrahamic religions are not at all anchored in an epistemic premise or a claim to special knowledge. The basis of these religions is rather found in Deuteronomy (6:4–6) in the famous *Shema Israel*. What does *shema* here mean? It is an invocation to the listeners to open their ears, not to harden their hearts, or to become "buffered selves." What are they to hear? Only this: that the Lord God is one and that "you should love the Lord with all your heart, with all your soul, and with all your might" and that this plea should dwell "upon your heart."

So the appeal here is to the heart rather than the head, to the whole human being rather than the knowing "subject." This appeal or plea is extended in Leviticus (19:18) where listeners are exhorted to love neighbors (or fellow beings) "as yourself." As we know, Jesus explicitly accepted these two kinds of love—which ultimately are one—and even affirmed that on these two pleas "depend all the law and the prophets" (Matthew 22:40). Clear echoes of the great *Shema*, however, can also be found in the Qur'an, which speaks of the need for humans to love the divine and to extend a similar love to each other. Likewise, the Hindu text Bhagavad Gita exhorts followers to bond with the divine through *yoga* and also to implement this bonding through interhuman service. And in Buddhism, compassion and ethical-spiritual service are meant to assist in the "awakening" of all creatures even beyond the interhuman domain.[11]

Given their concrete "existential" appeal, the language commonly used in religious texts is an ordinary language readily accessible to people in all walks of life and at all times; it is not a highly esoteric idiom tailored for theologians and hence in need of vernacular filtering. As it happens, this aspect was emphasized by Moses at the very time when he announced the divine laws. "This commandment which I announce to you this day," he said (Deuteronomy 30:11–14), is not too hard for you, nor is it far off. It is not in heaven so that you might say: "Who will go up for us to heaven and bring it to us, that we may hear it and do it?" Neither is it beyond the sea so that you might say: "Who will go over the sea for us and bring it to us, that we may hear it and do it?" But the word is very near you: it is in your mouth and in your heart, so that you can do it.

Large portions of the Hebrew Bible are historical accounts—and these are surely accessible to ordinary readers without special expertise. And what about the Psalms? They seem to be addressed to the joys and sorrows, the delights and sufferings of "everyman" (or every person). Uplifting and brazing—and beyond the need for filtering devices—are the words of the first Psalm: "Blessed is the man [person] who walks not in the counsel of the wicked . . . but his delight is in the law [teaching] of the Lord." And everyone who has experienced trouble or misery in life is surely touched by the words of Psalm 23: "The Lord is my shepherd, I shall not want; he makes me lie down in green pastures. He leads me beside still waters; he restores my soul."

The Christian (or "New") Testament is likewise filled with many stories or narratives, and especially the central story of the birth, ministry, and suffering of Jesus. Throughout his ministry, Jesus himself tells many stories, usually in the form of parables accessible to ordinary listeners. What filtering device is really necessary to understand the parable of the "good Samaritan" (Luke 10:29–37): the story where two Jewish priests (of all people) piously pass by a person who was robbed and brutally beaten—but where that victim is picked up and cared for by a traveling Samaritan (who was not even a member of the Jewish community)? To be sure, the story was not told for mere entertainment but for instruction—on the question "who is my neighbor?" And what about the story about the rich man who will have difficulty entering the "kingdom of God" (Matthew 19:23)—a story told again not for entertainment but instruction. In his ministry, Jesus never proclaimed a doctrine or epistemic paradigm but simply taught by practical example. When, after Golgotha, two men encountered him and followed him to Emmaus, they did not recognize him through an epistemic formula but in the simple breaking of bread (Luke 24:30–31). And what is one to say about the Sermon on the Mount and the great "beatitudes"? Where in modern moral theory—from utilitarianism to Kantianism—can one find similarly stirring words, like these (Luke 6:20–22): "Blessed are you who are poor, for yours is the kingdom of God. Blessed are you that hunger now, for you shall be satisfied. Blessed are you who weep now, for you shall be comforted"?

If, in these words, there is a need for translation, it is not so much a linguistic as rather a practical translation, that is, the transfer of teachings into human and social life. Here the letter of James is exemplary, and again it is written in generally accessible language. Elaborating on the great *Shema* in Deuteronomy, James emphasizes that hearing or listening cannot just be a passive receptivity but involves active following. As he states (James 1:22–25): "But be doers of the word and not hearers only, deceiving your-selves." For, he adds, someone who remains entirely passive is like a person who glances at an image and soon forgets what she or he has seen. But someone who looks into divine teachings and their message—which is "the law of liberty"—and perseveres in an active fashion, "shall be blessed in his doing." In an effort to underscore this point, James continues (2:14–17): "What does it profit if someone says he has faith but has no works? Can faith alone save him?" His letter, to be sure, does not say that action with-out faith is sufficient or commendable; rather hearing and doing should go together. Giving an example, he adds that "Abraham our father was justified by his works"—although one should better say that "his faith was active in or along with his works, or faith was completed by his actions." Returning to the role of religious faith in action, James offers a memorable definition (1:27): Religion that is "pure and undefiled" means simply this: "to visit orphans and widows in their affliction, and to keep oneself unstained from the world."[12]

Post-Secularity and Politics

Going back to Habermas's essay of 2008, one can now see fairly clearly "what is missing": it is an awareness of the primacy of lived experience over cognition, of ordinary language over epistemic paradigms, or (more simply) of doing or practice over knowing. This lacking awareness involves the pos-tulate of a self-enclosed (or "buffered") epistemic grid which is immune from disturbing experiences. This deficit has practical-political implications. In a somewhat disarming way, Habermas's essay acknowledges the deficit, stating that "enlightened reason loses its grip on the images, preserved by religion, of the moral whole—of the Kingdom of God on earth—as a collectively binding ideal." The consequences of this loss are far-reaching. Under the sway of the modern rational paradigm, "practical reason [too] fails to fulfill its own vocation when it no longer has sufficient strength to awaken, and to keep awake, in the minds of secular subjects, an awareness of the violations of solidarity throughout the world, an awareness of what is missing, of what cries out to heaven." Unfortunately, Habermas's carefully guarded epistemic grid provides few if any resources to remedy the acknowledged deficit.[13]

Against this background, it seems appropriate and desirable to take another look at "post-secularity." Maybe the time has come to redefine the term in such a way as to extricate it from the grip of both secular rationalists and religious anti-secularists. As it seems to me, once the latter is done, a new meaning of post-secularity comes into view: namely, communal or political meaning endowed with a transformational quality. At this point, post-secularity comes to designate a move beyond a corrupt kind of secular or "worldly" politics oriented solely toward such aims as power, wealth, and selfish interest; by correcting these aberrations, the "post" of post-secularity becomes a goalpost pointing toward the pursuit of justice and the good life (which are the intrinsic aims of politics).

In his 2009 response in New York City, Charles Taylor seems to gesture in this direction when he speaks of a "new moral order" (what I would prefer to call an ethical mode of public life) embracing such qualities as the rights and liberties of members, the equality of status among them, and the consensual legitimacy of public rule. If this general orientation is kept in mind, he writes, then what are called secularist or post-secularist regimes should be conceived "not primarily as bulwarks against religion but as good faith attempts to secure" the qualities mentioned before. And this means that contemporary regimes have "to shape their institutional arrangements not just to remain true to a hallowed tradition but to enhance the basic goods to liberty and equality between basic beliefs" and their adherents.[14]

At this point, I believe, one needs to take a few more steps beyond Taylor's recommendations—which still cling too closely to "liberal" conventions in celebrating universal maxims and cognitive "beliefs." In view of the enormous ills besetting political regimes today—large-scale economic corruption, media manipulation, and exploitation—it appears timely to envisage a still more "radical redefinition of secularism" which resonates more fully with a prophetic idiom—of which religious tradition is replete. Returning again to the book of Deuteronomy, we find this exhortation (16:20): "Justice and only justice you shall follow, so that you may live." And the psalmist proclaims in a similar vein (37:28): "For the Lord loves justice; he will not forsake his saints." And if we turn again to the Qur'an, we find these lines: "O ye believe! Stand out firmly for justice as witness to God" (sura 4:135) and "Be just, for that is next to piety" (sura 5:8). Although couched in somewhat different (nonprophetic) language, similar exhortations can readily be found in non-Abrahamic religious traditions in South and East Asia. As the Malaysian scholar Chandra Muzaffar has correctly remarked: "Justice is the real goal of any religion. It is the mission of every prophet and the message of every scripture." Nor is the call to social justice narrowly restricted to "religious" texts: it figures prominently in classical and modern philosophical teachings about civic "virtues." In the words of Aristotle—words echoed in the writings of al-Farabi, Avicenna, and Mencius: "What we call just is whatever produces and maintains happiness or blessedness (*eudaimonia*) for the *whole* of a political community and its parts." And as Aristotle importantly adds: justice and other virtues are practiced not for an external benefit or profit, since happiness or well-being is a "choice worthy in itself."[15]

This redirection or redefinition of secularism has implications also for the general meaning of "post-secularity." Viewed under social and political auspices, post-secularity is no longer the monopoly of secularists with a troubled conscience or else of anti-secularists but becomes available as a term designating all people—religious or not—with a public conscience, a conscience stirring them toward justice and social reform. From this angle, cognitive beliefs of whatever kind become secondary or subordinated to orthopraxis. In this respect, I completely concur with religious scholar Karen Armstrong when she states: "I say that religion is not about believing things. It's ethical alchemy: it is about behaving in a way that changes you, that gives you intimations of holiness and sacredness." In making this statement, Armstrong has the support not only of upright proponents of secular praxis but also of passages in sacred scripture, passages which sketch a development radically different from the well-known positivist trajectory (from religion to metaphysics to science): namely, a path leading from cognition to practice, and from head to heart. The main passage can be found in Jeremiah (31:31–34), but its gist is repeated elsewhere:

> Behold, the days are coming, says the Lord, when I will make a new covenant with the house of Israel and the house of Judah, not like the covenant which I made with their fathers. . . . And this is the covenant: I will put my law within them, and I will write it upon their hearts, and I will be their God, and they shall

be my people. And no longer shall each man have to instruct his neighbor and brother saying, "Know the Lord," for they shall know me, from the least of them to the greatest.[16]

What this and similar biblical passages suggest is a slow maturation or seasoning, a willing turn of people toward social justice and truth without doctrinal inculcation or creedal manifestoes. Such a process does not lend itself to political platforms or ideological proclamations, and certainly cannot rely on coercion or make common cause with "top-down" interruption or disruption. In our time, this process can no longer be restricted to one locality, one society, or one nation but must extend to humanity seen as a global community of interactive and ethically engaged people. In this manner, the contours of a "post-secular" cosmopolis come into view—a condition in which the differences between cultures, creeds, and customs would not be erased but subordinated to a shared striving for justice and well-being. This cosmopolis would be neither a super state nor a military-industrial complex but only the emblem of a hope or promise sustaining ordinary human lives: the promise of the "city of peace."[17]

3

POST-SECULAR FAITH

Toward a Religion of Service

But I am among you as one who serves.

—Luke 22:27

Somewhere in the middle of his life, John Dewey penned a short tract titled "A Common Faith" in which he distinguished between organized "religion" and religiosity or a "religious" disposition. Whereas the former denotes a formal institution wedded to official doctrines and rituals, the latter involves practical conduct, an ethically and perhaps spiritually informed manner of leading one's life.[1] As one should note, Dewey did not so much reject "religion" per se as rather its tendency to sideline lived experience or to privilege orthodoxy over orthopraxis. Despite changed circumstances, his tract on the whole has stood the test of time. Recent decades have seen the renewed upsurge of "religion" (in Dewey's sense), most often in the form of a reaffirmation of traditional doctrines or dogmas. Disturbingly, this kind of religion has made a comeback also in the political arena, a return which has been described as the "revenge of God." After having been exiled (at least in Western societies) from the public domain and confined to the field of private taste, religion in its various guises is suddenly back in the public limelight, with often unsettling consequences.

The return has elicited conflicting responses. For some observers—especially devotees of the modern liberal state—the upsurge of religion constitutes an assault on the basic acquisitions of modernity: principally the neutrality of the state, enlightened rationality, and the principle of religious freedom, that is, the freedom of individuals both for and from religion. For others—chiefly religious traditionalists—the upsurge signals a welcome renewal of the past, coupled with the defeat of modern Enlightenment and secular liberalism. In many contemporary debates, and especially in ongoing "culture wars," these two positions tend to monopolize the stage. However, there is the possibility—and this is the assumption that guides the following pages—that religion is indeed returning, but in a new or (what may be called) "post-secular" form, a form where religion, having traversed modern secularism, is freed from the hierarchical dross of the past.[2] This possibility—akin to Deweyan religiosity—heralds a new meaning of religious freedom and also the prospect of (what I shall call) a religion of service.

This prospect can be assessed in numerous ways, but also in terms of Max Weber's notion of "legitimacy." As is well known, Weber in his writings presents legitimacy as an "inner justification" which renders a given social and political order meaningful and acceptable in a durable sense. As a historical sociologist, he differentiates several types of such justification—among which I select only two. Premodern or traditional societies, in his view, were held together by "traditional legitimacy" anchored in (what he calls) "the authority of the 'eternal yesterday,'" that is, the mores and religious beliefs sanctified by their age and presumably sacred origin. A dramatic change occurred with the onset of modernity (in the West), a change which sidelined mores and religious beliefs in favor of the pure "legality" of a given regime. At this point, a public order is seen as legitimated—we might say: "thinly" legitimated—by virtue of the "validity of legal statutes," a validity deriving from the assumption that rules are "rationally established by enactment, contract, or imposition."[3] Broadly speaking, this "legal" kind of justification forms the bedrock of the modern secular "law state" (*Rechtsstaat*), where older mores and beliefs retreat into the privacy of psychic tastes. The question which arises here, and which Weber did not consider, is whether the bifurcation of public and private spheres is viable in the long run—which leads to the further query whether perhaps a "post-secular" religiosity or a new "common faith" is emerging, making room for a novel form of legitimacy.

To explore these questions I proceed in three steps. First, I examine lectures presented by Dewey's fellow pragmatist William James on the topic of "religious experience," together with a recent discussion of these lectures by Charles Taylor. As will be seen, the difference between premodern and modern forms of justification is transposed in Taylor's discussion into a Durkheimian vocabulary. In a second step, I introduce a distinction between modes of religious faith which, although indebted to James, moves beyond Jamesian individualistic psychology: the distinction between a religion of authority or mastery and a religion or religiosity of service. By way of conclusion, I reflect on the implications of this distinction for contemporary domestic and global politics.

Varieties of Religious Experience

Over a hundred years ago (in 1901–1902), William James presented his Gifford Lectures on "The Varieties of Religious Experience" in Edinburgh. At that time, psychology had just established itself as a new mode of inquiry and was attracting broad attention among both European and American intellectuals. This background is important for an understanding of the lectures. As a psychologist, albeit a very philosophical psychologist, James regarded religion basically as a mode of psychic experience—or as the name for a variety of psychic experiences—rather than a theological doctrine or official creed. As he confesses in his preface, a possible title of his lectures—one he later abandoned—was "man's religious appetites."

The opening lecture is even more explicit in this respect. Disclaiming any expertise as a theologian or "a scholar learned in the history of religions," James presents psychology as "the only branch of learning in which I am particularly versed"—a competence which suggested as the proper theme of his lectures a "descriptive survey of religious propensities." The second lecture goes a step further by spelling out the meaning of such phrases as "religious propensities" or "religious sentiments" and identifying the latter as particular "states of mind." "As concrete states of mind, made up of a feeling *plus* a specific sort of object," we read, "religious emotions, of course, are psychic entities distinguishable from other concrete emotions"—although there is no ground to assume a uniform sense of "religious emotion."[4] With these statements and elaborations, James clearly showed himself as a "modernist" concerned mainly with the inwardness of religious feeling rather than its broader social role—although the lectures' overall thrust was to rescue religious sentiment from neglect and to vindicate its general relevance.

The "inward" orientation is underscored and corroborated in subsequent passages of the lectures. Basically, James divides religion, or the phenomena characterizing the "religious field," into two broad branches: "On the one side . . . lies institutional, on the other personal religion"; the former branch keeps "the divinity," the second "man" uppermost in view. In the first branch,

James lumps together a host of practices, customs, and formal settings: "worship and sacrifice, procedures for working on the dispositions of the deity, theology and ceremony and ecclesiastical organization"—all features which, in his view, define religion as "an external art, the art of winning the favor of the gods." What James's comments here seem to anticipate, in an uncanny way, is Max Weber's notion of "traditional legitimacy" predicated on established beliefs and habitual forms of doing things—although his own concerns are far removed from questions of legitimacy. What matters to the psychologist is not the external dross but the domain of privately inward feeling—a domain set free by modernity and the consequences of the Reformation. Despite the persistence of some "outward" or traditional features on a subsidiary level, the accent in modern times has dramatically shifted. "The acts to which this sort of religion prompts," we read, "are personal not ritual acts; the individual transacts the business by himself alone, and the ecclesiastical organization, with its priests and sacraments and other go-betweens, sinks to an altogether secondary place"—making room for a religious feeling moving directly "from heart to heart, from soul to soul." Stressing further the inward outlook—and sidelining even further questions of public legitimacy—James defines the core of personal religion as involving "the feelings, acts, and experiences of individual men in their solitude, so far as they apprehend themselves to stand in relation to whatever they may consider the divine."[5]

About a hundred years after James's lectures, the Canadian philosopher Charles Taylor took up the leads contained in the former's arguments, in an effort to pinpoint their relevance or significance in our own secular or post-secular age. Curiously, the initial impulse was another set of Gifford Lectures presented by Taylor in 1999—in the course of which he encountered anew the work of his predecessor and decided to offer some of his own reflections or afterthoughts. (A brief version of these reflections—to which I limit myself here—was published in 2002 under the title *Varieties of Religion Today: William James Revisited*.) As one should note right away, Taylor's comments are not a pliant *explication de texte*. Although genuinely appreciative of James's work, the point of the "revisitation" is critical and reconstructive.

As the very first page tells us, James had "certain blind spots in his view of religion"—blind spots which are "widespread in the modern world." The main blind spot troubling Taylor is the narrow accent on individual feeling and personal or private inwardness. "James," Taylor writes, "sees religion primarily as something that individuals experience." Hence he makes a sharp divide "between living religious experience, which is that of the individual, and religious life, which is derivative because it is taken over from a community or church." Particularly troubling in this context is the core definition of personal religion (cited earlier) with its accent on "the feelings, acts and experiences of individual men in their solitude." What is completely blended out in this definition is the role of churches and religious communities. Thus, a central facet of the Jamesian approach, Taylor observes, is the role of experience or feeling set over "against the formulations by which people define, justify, rationalize their feelings" (operations frequently undertaken by churches).[6]

To some readers, Taylor's critical qualms might suggest a nostalgic traditionalism—which would be far off the mark. Although respectful of churches, Taylor is fully aware of the danger of "corporate" or "dogmatic dominion" and strongly in sympathy with the historical trend (in the West) toward individual religious freedom. His text offers a captivating overview of the main manifestations of this trend (an overview differing sharply from the story of religious decline depicted by Carl Schmitt in his *Political Theology*). As he notes, at least since the late Middle Ages, we can see in Western societies "a steadily increasing emphasis on a religion of personal commitment and devotion over forms centered on collective ritual." Evident initially in devotional movements and associations closely linked with the church, the trend reached a new stage with the Reformation, which, by insisting on salvation through faith alone (*sola fide*), had the effect of radically devaluing "ritual and external practices in favor of inward adherence to Christ as Savior." Subsequently, the same tendency was picked up by the Counter-Reformation, which spawned devotional movements of its own and proceeded to regulate the lives of believers along higher levels of inward commitment. Viewed against this background, James's "take on religion"—in Taylor's account—appears to be quite "in line with our modern understanding," which stipulates that, to take religion seriously, means "to take it personally, more devotionally, inwardly, more committedly."[7]

In an effort to provide sociological scaffolding to the sketched historical trend, Taylor turns mainly to Émile Durkheim, and especially the latter's *The Elementary Forms of Religious Life*.[8] As he notes, religion for Durkheim was basically a collective undertaking, a "life-form" where religion furnishes society with ultimate meaning by correlating mundane arrangements and sacred significance. In its traditional meaning, religion supported something like an "enchanted world," a world where God was seen as present in society, namely, "in the loci of the sacred." This view carried distinct political connotations. As Ernst Kantorowitz has shown, in earlier societies kingdoms existed "not only in ordinary, secular time" but also "in higher times," thus endowing the king with "two bodies." Later periods brought a growing "disenchantment" (in Max Weber's sense). Metaphysically speaking, Taylor observes, "there was a shift from the enchanted world [of the past] to a cosmos conceived in conformity with post-Newtonian science," a cosmos regulated and held together by natural laws. To the extent that it persisted, religious belief—rather than finding the sacred in the world—now construed it as a transcendent principle, relegating God to the role of a distant "designer" or architect of the world. In social and political terms, this change translated into a society of individual designers or entrepreneurs, fashioning social life contractually in accordance with general laws (or the designs of "nature's God"). In large measure, this vision inspired the modern nation-state seen as a "law state" (*Rechtsstaat*) coupling higher norms with individual rights. In more recent times, this precarious "synthesis" gave way to (what Taylor calls) the "new individualism" of late modernity.[9]

Simplifying his historical account somewhat, Taylor introduces a number of variations on the Durkheimian conception of "religious life." Basically, three such variations are juxtaposed in the manner of ideal types: a "paleo-Durkheimian," a "neo-Durkheimian," and a "post-Durkheimian" dispensation or arrangement. The first type corresponds in essence to the traditionalist understanding of religion as the warrant of an "enchanted" world and emblem of a divinely sanctioned authority structure. "Under the paleo-Durkheimian dispensation," we read, "my connection to the sacred entailed my belonging to a church, in principle coextensive with society"—a church representative of "higher times" or a divine order. The second or "neo-Durkheimian" dispensation refers to the coexistence of religion and society in the modern state where a "neutral" or procedural framework makes room for a variety of churches, denominations, and sects. In this neo-Durkheimian mode, Taylor states, we find "an important step toward the individual and the right of choice. One joins a denomination because it seems right to one"—although there is still a pervasive sense that all choices are somehow held together by a broader, divinely designed architecture. This assumption erodes or vanishes in the "non-" or "post-Durkheimian" setting inaugurated or unleashed by the "new individualism." At this point, the last traces of social "holism" and a unified church structure give way to a radical celebration of private inwardness. Differently phrased: belief of any kind is privatized and detached from social-political contexts: "In our post-Durkheimian dispensation, the 'sacred,' either religious or 'laïque,' is uncoupled from our political allegiance."[10]

Returning to the lectures of his famous predecessor, Taylor places William James (perhaps too quickly) in the context of an emerging post-Durkheimian world. Although separated from us by a century, he notes, James is "very close to the spirit of contemporary society" in that he was "already living in his own post-Durkheimian dispensation." The basic question animating Taylor's text could be put in this manner: Has the new individualism really succeeded in erasing all modes of religious or spiritual holism? Differently phrased: Does the accent on "personal religion"—while valuable as a crucial harbinger of religious freedom—really preclude the possibility of shared religious practices in a social and political community? Properly pursued, this question brings into view the contours of a "post-secular" (rather than post-Durkheimian) society and with it the prospect of a post-secular mode of public legitimacy. Without using the latter terminology, Taylor at least gestures in that direction. As a philosopher, he is supported in this post-individualist move by the so-called "linguistic turn"—the emphasis on shared languages inaugurated by Wittgenstein, Heidegger, and others—and by the so-called "decentering of the subject" promoted by post-structuralist writings. If these initiatives are well grounded, would they not necessarily have effects on religious life as well? In Taylor's words: Although the modern intellectual trajectory has a strongly inward or "individualist component," does this necessarily mean or entail that the content of belief will be "individuating"?[11]

At another point of his text, Taylor ventures still a bit further into the terrain of a post-secular religiosity. Suppose, he argues (I freely paraphrase), that we do not wish to return to the constraints of a "paleo-Durkheimian" collectivism. Suppose we wish to have no truck with the bigotries of "corporate" or "dogmatic dominion" of the past and prefer to celebrate—with James—the modern trend toward inwardness as a gateway to religious freedom: Does this attitude really confine us to "experiences of individual men in their solitude"? Does an inwardly cultivated religious commitment not rather stimulate the desire to share our lives with other people and to participate in their joys and agonies? In the Hegelian terminology familiar to James, is there not ample room for transitions, linkages, and mediations? Let us imagine, Taylor writes, that a religious calling—or the demand laid upon as by God—is not so much a call to solitude as rather a call to service? Let us further imagine that what we are asked to do is "to live together in brotherly love, and to radiate outward such love as a community." If we accept this supposition, then the locus of religious life or of our "relation with God" is—has to be—also "through the community, and not simply in the individual."[12] But if this is so, then the isolating post-Durkheimian setting gives way to a post-secular social setting in which religious belief can be again a resource of social responsibility and ethical legitimacy.

Toward a Religion of Service

Apart from discussing James's work, Taylor's text points in the direction of a new social religiosity, perhaps a "common faith"—although his comments remain sketchy and brief. As it happens, he has fleshed out his views a bit more on other occasions; one such occasion was his Marianist Award Lecture of 1996 on the possibility of a "Catholic modernity." The central issue addressed in the lecture is whether a mode of religious commitment can be preserved in the modern and contemporary context—without succumbing to the "new individualism" or being confined to a privatized inwardness. As in the *Varieties* book, the answer for Taylor cannot be found in a simple return to the past, especially not the "paleo-Durkheimian" dispensation of traditional "Christendom" wedded to corporate or dogmatic dominion over people.

Such a return would cancel the entire modern trajectory toward personal belief and religious freedom, a trajectory which (in his view) has put an end to that "continual and often bloody forcing of conscience" which was the blight of so-called "Christian" centuries. The question remains, however, whether personal religion is necessarily limited—with (the early) James—to the feelings of "individual men in their solitude," or whether it can radiate out into social and public life in noncoercive ways, thereby regaining a "holistic" quality. Taylor clearly opts for the second alternative. A new Christian spirituality is emerging, he notes. It can be described "either as a love or compassion that is unconditional . . . or as one based on what you are most profoundly: a being in the image of God." In either case, the love is not predicated on "the worth realized in you just as an individual" or an isolated creature: "Our being in the image of God is also our standing among others in the stream of love"—which demands service to others.[13]

In many ways, Taylor's turn to a religiosity of service was anticipated by the French philosopher Paul Ricoeur in writings penned several decades ago. The starting point of Ricoeur's reflections was precisely the modern move toward privatization and religious inwardness—a move which he both welcomed as a gateway to religious freedom and criticized as a possible retreat or exodus of faith from the world and social concerns. As he wrote hopefully in an essay of 1958: "After several centuries during which Christians have been preoccupied with the inner life and personal salvation, we are discovering afresh what is meant by 'you are the salt of the earth' (Matthew 5:13). We are discovering that the salt is made for salting, the light for illuminating, and that the church exists for the sake of those outside itself."

Like Taylor later, Ricoeur was not enamored with the "paleo-Durkheimian" arrangement where church and faith exert a dominant (quasi-sovereign) political control in society. Despite the long historical trajectory toward freedom, he noted, the old dispensation still tends to assert or reassert itself in many guises. There is still a widespread illusion that religion can play "a direct political role as an independent political power"—an illusion (often coupled with hypocrisy) which manifests itself in the pretense of so-called "Christian" governments, "Christian" parties, or "Christian" policies. But another alternative is possible: "When it emerges from this illusion, the church will be able to give light once more to all men—no longer as a power, but as a prophetic message." Giving light to all men means also to serve, guard, and rescue. "Christian love," Ricoeur adds, "consists in seeking out the fresh forms of poverty which occur at any period" (where poverty includes all forms of deprivation, oppression, and injustice). Today, in our globalizing age, it must "direct its attention toward the great world problems."[14]

In the meantime, the critique of religious mastery in the paleo-Durkheimian mode has spread from isolated remonstrations to broader intellectual endeavors, including theology, philosophy of religion, and (even) political philosophy. In the theological domain, the critique finds resonance in a current of thought aiming to shift the emphasis from a sovereign (possibly imperial) creator God to the legacy of the "suffering servant" extolled by Deutero-Isaiah, a legacy sometimes linked with the notion of a "co-suffering" of God with the world.[15] In some respects, this shift joins hands with another perspective called "liberation theology," characterized by an accent on "exodus" from unjust power structures and a "preferential" engagement for the poor.[16]

Similar tendencies are present in contemporary philosophy of religion, a field strongly marked by the intellectual upheavals associated with Nietzsche and his "post-modern" followers. Thus, distancing himself from the notion of divine omnipotence, philosopher John Caputo speaks provocatively of the "weakness of God"—where "weakness" does not denote impotence but rather the recessed quality of divine calling. "I treat God," Caputo writes, "not as an eminent omnipotent power capable of leveling tall buildings and reducing his enemies to ashes, but as the weak force of a call." This weak force of God, he adds, "is to lay *claim* upon us . . . but not the way

a sovereign power . . . invades and then lays claim to a territory, over-
powers its native population and plants a foreign flag, but in the way of
a summons that calls and provokes, an appeal that incites or invites us, a
promise that awakens our love."[17] In a similar way, Richard Kearney speaks
of the "powerlessness" of divine empowerment, stating: "By choosing to be
a player rather than an emperor of creation, God chooses powerlessness," a
choice which "expresses itself as self-emptying, *kenosis*, letting go." God, he
adds, thus "empowers our human powerlessness by giving away his power,
by possibilizing us and our good actions—so that we may supplement and
co-accomplish creation."[18]

Somewhat surprisingly—because of the usual association of politics
with power—the critique of the religion of mastery also surfaces today in
versions of political theory or philosophy. For purposes of illustration I
choose the theorist William Connolly because his writings fully resonate
with this critique—and also reconnect us again with the work of William
James. In his book titled *Pluralism*, Connolly pays tribute to James as the
author not only of *The Varieties of Religious Experience* but also of *A Pluralistic Universe*—a text penned a few years after his Gifford Lectures. For
Connolly, James was a pioneering thinker who, ahead of many others, was
able to articulate modern (and perhaps post-modern) sensibilities not by
relying on abstract categories but by turning to concretely lived experience.

In pursuing this path, he was a partner of Henri Bergson and Dewey,
and a precursor of such later thinkers as Wittgenstein, Heidegger, and
Merleau-Ponty. His turn to concrete experience prompted James to reject
the notion of a fully mapped, totally transparent, and rationally intelligible
cosmos. As he wrote in *A Pluralistic Universe*: "The substance of reality
may never get totally collected, . . . some of it may remain outside of the
largest combination of it ever made."[19] The inference Connolly draws from
this statement is that "there is no omnipotent, omniscient God outside or
above the world who gathers all of the universe together into one system of
intelligible relations—though there may be a limited God who participates
as one important actor among others in the world." The pluralistic view
sponsored by James, one should note, does not entail an endorsement of
radical chaos, fragmentation, or chance—which would be another abstract
and totalizing maxim. Rather, fragmentary elements and sensations are already
linked, though in unmappable and often surprising ways: "The Jamesian idea
is that sensations, set in the protracted pulse of time in which they occur,
arrive already equipped with a set of preliminary connections."[20]

In the domain of religious faith, Connolly together with James opposes the idea of a sovereign, imperial deity—a stance which leads him also to critique recent attempts to restore paleo-Durkheimian arrangements in the West. Addressing some fellow theorists overly nostalgic of the past, he chides their hankering for a religion of mastery manifest in an "exclusionary, imperious sensibility," favoring the imposition of a uniform creed. In challenging dogmatic uniformity, Connolly does not mean to lend aid and comfort to the simple privatization of faith, to the neo-Durkheimian separation of the neutral state and the private inwardness of belief. As he observes in a striking formulation: defenders of liberal neutrality pretend to identify "a forum entirely above faith through which to regulate diverse faiths"—while ignoring "faith practices themselves." Hence, he adds, "if the nobility of secularism resides in its quest to enable multiple faiths to exist on the same public space, its shallowness resides in the hubris of its distinction between private faith and public reason."

By taking religious practices seriously, Connolly's book also departs from *The Varieties of Religious Experience* by transgressing the feelings of "solitary men" in the direction of shared religious engagements, a shared "post-secular" sensibility conducive to public legitimacy. "Deep pluralism," he writes, "reinstates the link between practice and belief that had been artificially severed by secularism; and it overturns the impossible counsel to bracket your faith when you participate in politics." In the best-case scenario, faith-imbued practices of devotion are joined with civic practices that instill "forbearance and presumptive generosity [toward others]" in social life. In this preferred situation, each faith is able to embed "the religious virtue of hospitality and the civic virtue of presumptive generosity into its relational practices."[21]

Multiple Faiths in a Shared World

Connolly's text is important here not only for its Jamesian sensibilities but also for its attention to multiple faith traditions and the desirability of fostering "generous" relations between them. His notion of a "deep" or "expansive" pluralism gains its acute significance precisely in the context of our globalizing and pluri-cultural world. "The most urgent need today," he writes, "is to mix presumptively generous sensibilities into a variety of theistic and nontheistic creeds, sensibilities attuned to the contemporary need to transfigure relations of antagonism between faiths into relations of agonistic respect." The point here is not to obliterate differences between faiths in a bland ecumenicism but to forge "a positive ethos of public engagement between alternative faiths."[22] The question often asked with regard to interfaith relations—especially relations animated by generosity—is whether mutual recognition is not purchased at too high a price: the price of the shallowness or lukewarmness of one's own faith commitment. Does navigating in the "pluriverse" of different faith traditions not necessarily erode the firmness of one's convictions and possibly lead to alienation from traditional faith practices? This question (it seems to me) is predicated on a basic antinomy between "vertical" and "horizontal" human relationships. In terms of this antinomy, only the vertical relation between humans and God is considered properly religious, while interhuman relations are devalued as secular, worldly, and possibly harmful to religious faith. The governing assumption is that of a "zero sum" game where the winnings of one side are the losses on the other side.

If interfaith relations really wish to get off the ground, this assumption has to be defeated, not just in theory but in practical life. A prominent exemplar of such lived practice is Jonathan Sacks, widely renowned as a religious leader, intellectual, writer, and peacemaker. Although intensely involved in interfaith relations, Sacks is not a shallow believer; he is an orthodox Jew and, in fact, the chief rabbi of the United Hebrew Congregations of Britain and the Commonwealth. Among his numerous writings, particularly relevant in the present context is his book *The Dignity of Difference* (published in 2002). Subtitled *How to Avoid the Clash of Civilizations*, the book seeks to make a contribution to interfaith harmony and, through it, to global peace. As Sacks writes in the opening pages: "One of the unexpected delights of becoming a religious leader has been the friendships I have made with leaders of other faiths, nationally and internationally," bonds which demonstrate that "the world's great faiths have a significant potential role in conflict resolution and not merely . . . in conflict creation." To advance and foster this role, something more is required than bland coexistence or even shallow tolerance among faiths. As the text makes clear, the author is speaking as a believing Jew, placing himself in the Jewish faith tradition. He is able to do this and yet also celebrate "difference" because Judaism has always been located at the cusp between particularism and globalism: "The book of Genesis was the first to see all humankind as bound by a universal covenant, and yet to acknowledge the legitimacy of profound religious and cultural differences." Hence, for Sacks, vertical and lateral or horizontal relations are not in conflict but supplement each other: "My primary aim has been to suggest a new paradigm for our complex, interconnected world, in such a way that, the more passionately we feel our religious commitment, the more space we make for those who are not like us."[23]

As one should note well, passionately held religious commitment here does not suggest a hankering for political power. Together with Taylor and Connolly, Sacks is not a devotee of paleo-Durkheimian dispositions or a religion of mastery—without at the same time favoring a retreat into privacy. As he writes: "Religious leaders should never seek power, but neither may they abdicate their task of being a counter-voice [or a voice resisting oppression and injustice] in the conversation of mankind." Together with Connolly, *The Dignity of Difference* celebrates a deep or expansive kind of pluralism; in several respects, however, it moves beyond the level of simple recognition or a (perhaps grudgingly granted) "agonistic respect." In a stunning formulation, Sacks articulates an idea which belongs to the core of a religion of service. A faith community, he writes, "should encourage its members to do an act of service or kindness to someone or some group of another faith or ethnicity—to extend a hand of help, in other words, *across* the boundaries of difference and thus turn communities outward instead of inward." As a believing Jew, Sacks invites members of other faith communities to join him in prayer; but prayer needs to be linked with action and practical engagement on behalf of the marginalized and persecuted.

In this respect, his text is again exemplary by counseling not mindless activism (in the service of possibly self-aggrandizing agendas) but rather engagement in response to a summons or call. Sacks at this point invokes the great biblical exhortation *Shema Israel*, where *shema* means "to hear, to understand and to respond, to listen in the fullest range of senses"—listen also and especially to the agonies of the suffering and oppressed. "I believe," he adds, "that God is summoning us to a new act of listening" today, involving above all caring attentiveness to some of the side effects of globalization: "its inequities, its consumerism and exploitation, its failure to address widespread poverty and disease, its juggernaut insensitivity to local traditions and cultures, and the spiritual poverty that can go hand in hand with material wealth."[24]

Religiously speaking, Sacks's account of what needs to happen is surely on solid ground. As we know, the central message of the biblical *Shema Israel* was the dual plea addressed to Jews, first, to love God or the divine with all their being, and secondly, to love their fellow beings in an equal manner (Deuteronomy 6:5; Leviticus 19:18). This dual plea was taken over almost verbatim in the Christian gospels (Matthew 22:37–40; Luke 10:27–28; Mark 12:29–31). Thus, Sacks in pleading for a religion of loving service speaks from the heart of at least two great faith traditions.

But the biblical *shema* is by no means alien to the Islamic tradition either. First of all, Islam does not cancel but builds upon the older foundations of Hebrew faith (including the passages in Deuteronomy and Leviticus). Secondly and still more importantly, the Qur'an itself resonates fully with the older biblical exhortations. Thus, sura 3 speaks of the human love for God—a love reciprocated and even anticipated by God's love for humans; while sura 90 speaks of interhuman love, which yields the demand or duty "to free a neck (from the burden of debt and slavery), or to feed in times of famine the orphan near in relationship or the poor in distress."[25]

In the Hindu faith tradition, the Bhagavad Gita portrays eloquently the vertical relation between humans and the divine as a mode of mutual bonding, stating: "In whatever way humans love me, in that same way they find my love." This bonding, however, is instantly joined with another, more lateral connection taking the form of "consecrated" action or interhuman service: "Let your aim be the good of all (*lokasamgraha*), and thus carry on your task in life." One hardly needs to make special mention here of the central role of compassion and ethical-spiritual service in Buddhism, a tradition exhorting its followers to strive for the awakening and "liberation" of all sentient creatures "however innumerable they may be."[26]

Sacred scriptures and holy texts, however, are dead letters unless they are taken up by real-life people and translated into appropriate action in a concrete time and place. In our own time, the concrete context is marked by globalization including global militarism and worldwide "terror wars." Given the dominant view that in politics—especially international politics—power and security always trump ethics and religion, faith-based traditions face an uphill struggle in trying to have their voices heard. Fortunately, even today there are courageous people able and willing to "speak truth (especially religious truth) to power"; among them I want to lift up for consideration Richard Falk, well known for his work on international politics.

In a recent essay on "religious resurgence" in our "era of globalization," Falk soberly but hopefully assesses the prospect of a faith-based transformation of prevailing political practices in the world. As an expert in this field, he is fully aware of the obstacles facing this prospect. As he writes: "The religious dimension of human experience has been generally excluded from the serious study and practice of governance for several centuries, especially in the West." Experiences of the last two centuries, however—world wars,

Holocaust, and genocides—have revealed the limitations or dark downsides of modern "disenchantment," thus triggering a return to recessed and previously sidelined religious resources. As Falk makes abundantly clear, his trust is not placed in revivalist triumphalism or any paleo-Durkheimian arrangements. "In many occasions," he acknowledges, "the religious establishment of the day defends the status quo, and is itself part of the oppressive social and political order." Too often, established religious institutions find the visions of reformers unsettling and disruptive and hence "tend to marginalize their impact." As against this Durkheimian model, Falk joins James and Taylor in embracing a more inward and personal mode of religiosity practiced in everyday life: "Religion is understood here as encompassing not only the teachings, beliefs, and practices of organized religions but all spiritual outlooks that interpret the meaning of life by reference to faith"; in this sense, religion includes "belief in God and gods, but does not depend on theistic convictions, or for that matter, theological dogma of any kind."[27]

As in the case of Taylor and Ricoeur—one needs to add—cultivation of personal religiosity for Falk does not signal retreat into solitude but rather radiates out into the world. In an eloquent formulation which captures the gist of (what I have called) a religion of service, Falk writes: "A belief in the transformative capacities of an idea that is sustained by spiritual energy lends itself to nonviolent forms of struggle and sacrifice, thereby challenging most secular views of human history as shaped primarily by governing elites, warfare, and a command over innovative military technology." Despite certain differences of emphasis, Falk's outlook in this respect resonates fully with Jonathan Sacks's construal of religion as a response to a divine *shema* or exhortation: the call to justice. "The religious framing of reality," Falk notes, "is rooted in the present, but is also hopeful about deliverance from suffering and privation. Indeed, the central founding narratives of the world's great religions are preoccupied with liberation from oppressive social and political arrangements, promising that by adhering to faith, emancipation will be attained."

Looking at our contemporary global situation, Falk finds abundant evidence of the need for transformative liberation from injustice or oppression. In all domains of social life today, he observes, one finds an immense concentration of privilege: the privilege of wealth, power, and expertise. To redress this imbalance is a religious and ethical demand—but one requiring sustained effort. Soberly assessed, transformation today "will occur only as the outcome of human struggle," which in this sense is "similar to past efforts to overcome slavery, colonialism, and apartheid." The greatest stumbling block for transformation resides, he states, in a renewed imperialist agenda, the attempt to erect a uniform super-Leviathan governing the world. "Only the great world religions," Falk concludes (and I fully concur), "have the credibility and legitimacy to identify and reject the idolatry that seems to lie at the core of this project of planetary domination."[28] Eloquently formulated, we find here the prospect of a post-secular legitimacy.

4

BEYOND SECULAR MODERNITY

Reflections on Taylor and Panikkar

Why do you stand looking into heaven?

—Acts 1:11

At least in the Western context, our age is commonly referred to as that of "modernity"—a term sometimes qualified as "late modernity" or "post-modernity." Taken by itself, the term is nondescript; in its literal sense, it simply means a time of novelty or innovation. Hence, something needs to be added to capture the kind of novelty involved. To pinpoint this innovation, modernity is also referred to as the "age of reason" or the age of enlightenment and science—in order to demarcate the period from a prior age presumably characterized by unreason, metaphysical speculation, and intellectual obscurantism or darkness. Seen in this light, modernity for a large number of people—including supporters of scientific and social progress—is a cause for rejoicing, celebration, and unrelenting promotion. As is well known, however, this chorus of support has for some time been accompanied by discordant voices pointing to the dark underside of modernity, evident in what Max Weber called the "disenchantment" of the world and others (more dramatically) the "death of God" or the "flight of the gods." More recently, discontent has given rise to claims regarding an inherent "crisis" of modernity manifest in the slide toward materialism, consumerism, irreligion, and a general "loss of meaning."[1]

For present purposes I want to lift up for consideration two highly nuanced and philosophically challenging assessments of our modern condition: Charles Taylor's *A Secular Age* (of 2007) and Raimon Panikkar's *The Rhythm of Being* (of 2010). As it happens, both texts are strongly revised versions of earlier Gifford Lectures (presented, respectively, in 1999 and 1989).

Before proceeding, a word of caution: neither of the two thinkers belongs to one of the polarized camps—which means that neither is an uncritical "booster" or else a mindless "knocker" of the modern age.[2] Both thinkers share many things in common. Both complain about certain glaring blemishes of the modern, especially the contemporary period; both deplore above all a certain deficit of religiosity or spirituality. The differences between the two authors have to do mainly with the details of their diagnosis and proposed remedies. In Taylor's view, the modern age—styled as "secular age"—appears marked by a slide into worldly agnosticism, into "exclusive humanism," and above all into an "immanent fame" excluding or marginalizing theistic "transcendence." Although sharing the concern about "loss of meaning," Panikkar does not find its source in the abandonment of (mono)theistic transcendence; nor does he locate this source in secularism or "secularity" per se—seeing that, in view of its temporality, faith is necessarily linked with a given age (or *saeculum*). Instead of stressing the dichotomy between immanence and transcendence, Panikkar focuses on the pervasive "oblivion of being" in our time, an oblivion which can only be overcome through a renewed remembrance of the divine as a holistic happening in a "cosmotheandric" mode.

A Secular Age

At the very beginning of his massive study, Taylor distinguishes between three kinds of secularity or "the secular": "secularity 1" involving the retreat of faith from public life; "secularity 2" denoting a diminution or vanishing of faith among certain people; and "secularity 3" involving the erosion of the very conditions of possibility of shared faith. While in the first type, public spaces are assumed to be "emptied of God, or of any reference to ultimate reality," and whereas in the second type secularity consists "in the falling off of religious belief and practice, in people turning away from God," the third type involves a more pervasive change: namely, "a move from a society where belief in God is unchallenged and indeed, unproblematic, to one in which it is understood to be one option among others, and frequently not the easiest to embrace." Taken in the third sense, secularity means more than the evacuation of public life or else the loss of a personal willingness to believe; rather, it affects "the whole context of understanding in which our moral, spiritual or religious experience and search takes place." Viewed on this level, an age or a society would be secular or not "in virtue of the conditions of experience of and search for the spiritual." As Taylor emphasizes, the focus of his study is on the last kind of secularity. In his words:

> So I want to examine our society as secular in this third sense, which I could perhaps encapsulate in this way: the change I want to define and trace is one which takes us from a society in which it was virtually impossible not to believe in God, to one in which faith, even for the staunchest believer, is one human possibility among others. Belief in God is no longer axiomatic.[3]

In seeking to flesh out the meaning of secularity as a mode of modern experience, Taylor's text very quickly introduces the notion of "exclusive humanism" or "self-sufficient humanism" characterized by a neglect of transcendence. An important criterion here is the notion of a "fullness of life" and whether this fullness can be reached by human resources alone or requires a step "beyond" or "outside." "The big obvious contrast here," we read, "is that for believers the account of the place of fullness requires reference to God, that is, something beyond human life and/or nature; where for unbelievers this is not the case." Typically, for believers, fullness or completion is received as a gift whereas for unbelievers the source of completion resides "within." Appeal to internal resources can take many forms. In modernity, the appeal is frequently to the power of reason and rational knowledge. However, self-sufficiency can also be predicated on a "rigorous naturalism." In that case, the sources of fullness are not transcendent but are to be "found in Nature, or in our own inner depths, or in both." Examples of such naturalism are provided by "the Romantic critique of disengaged reason, and most notably certain ecological ethics of our day, particularly deep ecology." Other forms of self-sufficiency or internal self-reliance can be found in versions of Nietzscheanism and existentialism which draw empowerment "from the sense of our courage and greatness in being able to face the irremediable, and carry on nonetheless." A further modality can be detected in recent modes of post-modernism which, while dismissive of claims of self-sufficient reason, yet "offer no outside source for the reception of power."[4]

In subsequent remarks the distinction between inside and outside ("within-without") is further sharpened by the invocation of the binaries of immanence/transcendence and natural/supernatural. "The shift in background, or better the disruption of the earlier background," Taylor writes, "comes best to light when we focus on certain distinctions we make today: for instance, that between the immanent and the transcendent, the natural and the super-natural. It is this shift in background, in the whole context in which we experience and search for fullness, that I am calling the coming of a secular age, in my third sense [and] that I want to describe, and perhaps also (very partially) explain." In general terms, modernity for Taylor assumes the character of a "secular age" once priority is granted to immanence over transcendence and to a self-sufficient humanism over divine interventions. "The great invention of the [modern] West," he writes, "was that of an immanent order of Nature whose working could be systematically understood and explained on its own terms." This notion of immanence involves denying, or at least questioning, "any form of interpenetration between the things of Nature, on the one hand, and the 'supernatural,' on the other." Seen from this angle, he adds, "defining religion in terms of the distinction immanent/transcendent is a move tailor-made for our culture." From a humanist perspective, the basic question becomes "whether people recognize something beyond or transcendent to their lives."[5]

At the core of the modern secular shift, for Taylor, is the issue of human fulfillment or "flourishing," that is, the question "what constitutes a fulfilled life?" At this point, an intriguing radicalism comes to the fore: in the sense that not only the secular goals of fulfillment are chastised, but the very idea of human flourishing is called into question. In earlier periods, he comments, it was still possible to assume that the best life involved our seeking "a good which is beyond, in the sense of being independent of human flourishing." In that case, the highest, most adequate human striving could include our aiming "at something other than human flourishing." Under the aegis of an exclusive or self-sufficient humanism, the possibility of such higher striving has atrophied and even vanished. Differently phrased: "secularity" in Taylor's sense came along together with the possibility and even probability of exclusive humanism. In fact, he states, one could offer this "one-line description" of the difference between earlier times and the secular age: "a secular age is one in which the eclipse of all goals beyond human flourishing becomes conceivable." Here is the crucial link "between secularity and a self-sufficing humanism." In traditional religion, especially in Christianity, a different path was offered: namely, "the possibility of transformation . . . which takes us beyond merely human perfection." To follow this path, it was needful to rely on "a higher power, the transcendent God." Seen in this light, Christian faith requires "that we see our life as going beyond the bounds of its 'natural' scope between birth and death; our lives extend beyond 'this life.'"[6]

It cannot be my ambition here to recapitulate Taylor's complex and lengthy tome; suffice it for present purposes to draw attention briefly to a central chapter dealing with the noted binary tension, the chapter titled "The Immanent Frame." At this point, the notion of an exclusive human-ism is reformulated in terms of a "buffered self." According to Taylor, what modern secularity chiefly entails is "the replacement of a porous self by the buffered self," a self that begins to find "the idea of spirits, moral forces, causal powers with a purposive bent, close to incomprehensible." Buffering here involves "interiorization," that is, a withdrawal into "an inner realm of thought and feeling to be explored." Examples of this inward turn are said to be Romanticism, the "ethic of authenticity," and similar moves prompting us to "conceive ourselves as having inner depths." A corollary of this turn is "the atrophy of earlier ideas of cosmic order" and the rise of individual self-reliance and self-development, especially of an "instrumental individualism" exploiting worldly resources to its own exclusive benefit. Aggregating the various changes or mutations occurring in secular moder-nity, Taylor arrives at this succinct formulation: "So, the buffered identity of the disciplined [self-reliant] individual moves in a constructed social space, where instrumental rationality is a key value and time is pervasively secular [as clock time]. All of this makes up what I want to call 'the immanent frame.'" There is one important background feature which also needs to be taken into account: namely, that "this frame constitutes a 'natural' order, to be contrasted to a 'supernatural' one, an immanent world over against a possible 'transcendent' one."[7]

As Taylor recognizes, the boundary between the two "worlds" is not always sharply demarcated. Although ready to "slough off the transcendent," the immanent order occasionally makes concessions to the former. This happens in various forms of "civil region" and also in vaguely spiritual movements or expressions like Pentecostalism or "Romantic forms of art." However, such concessions are at best half-hearted and do not basically challenge or impede the "moral attraction" of immanence, of this-worldli-ness, of materialism and naturalism. As Taylor remarks with regard to the latter: "We can see in the naturalistic rejection of the transcendent . . . the ethical outlook which pushes to closure" in immanence, especially when the rejection is coupled with a wholesale trust in modern natural science and associated technologies. Undergirded by this trust, the entire growth of modern civilization can be seen "as synonymous with the laying out of a closed immanent frame." To be sure, the text insists, the "moral attraction" of immanence is not absolutely compelling or preordained; it only prevails as a dominant pull or possibility, leaving room for other recessed alternatives. Resisting the dominant frame, some individuals find themselves placed in the cauldron of competing pulls—a cauldron giving rise sometimes to the striving for a radical exodus, accomplished through a stark (Kierkegaardian) "leap of faith." However, this personal experience of cross-pressures does not call into question the basic structure of secular modernity. What his study is trying to bring to the fore, Taylor concludes, is the "constitution of [secular] modernity" in terms of the emphasis on " 'closed' or 'horizontal' worlds," which leave little or no place for "the 'vertical' or 'transcendent.' "[8]

Without doubt, Taylor's *A Secular Age* is an intellectual tour de force as well as a spirited defense of religious faith (seen as openness to a transcendent realm). In an age submerged in the maelstrom of materialism, consumerism, and mindless self-indulgence, his book has the quality of a wake-up call, of a stirring plea for transformation and *metanoia*. Nevertheless, even while appreciating the cogency of this plea, the reader cannot quite escape the impression of a certain one-dimensionality. Despite repeated rejections of a "subtraction story" (treating modernity simply as a culture minus faith), the overall account presented in the book is one of diminution or impoverishment: leading from a holistic framework hospitable to transcendence to an "immanent frame" hostile to it. Surely, this is not the only story that can be told—and probably not the most persuasive one. In Taylor's presentation, immanence and transcendence, this world and the world "beyond," seem to be immutable binary categories exempt from change. Clearly, there is the possibility of another (more compelling) narrative: a story where immanence and transcendence, the human and the divine, encounter each other in ever new ways, leading to profound transformations on both (or all) sides. Curiously, Taylor's own earlier writings had been leaning more in that direction. One of his best-known earlier works, *Sources of the Self*, narrated the development of human selfhood from antiquity to modernity in a nuanced manner not reducible to a slide from porousness to buffered closure. Very little of this story remains in *A Secular Age*. In a similar manner, the "ethics of authenticity" (highlighted in one of his earlier books) now seems to be just another synonym for modern buffering and self-sufficiency. Even the move toward personal religiosity—celebrated earlier in the case of William

James—now seems to be relegated to a marginal gloss on the "immanent frame." Hardly an echo seems to be left of the "thanks to Voltaire and others"—extended in his "Marianist Lecture"—for "allowing us to live the gospel in a purer way," free of the "often bloody forcing of conscience" marking previous centuries.[9]

As it seems to me, one of the more curious and troubling aspects of the book is the determined privileging of the "vertical" or "transcendent" dimension over the lateral or "horizontal worlds." Even if one were to grant the atrophy of transcendence, modernity styled as a "secular age" surely has witnessed important "horizontal," social-political developments by no means alien to a religious register: the demolition of ancient caste structures, the struggles against imperialism, the emancipation of slaves, the steady process of democratization promising equal treatment for people without regard for gender, race, and religion. Strangely, in a book seeking to distill the essence of Western modernity, these and similar developments occupy a minor or shadowy place, being eclipsed by the accent on verticality (heavily indebted to certain monotheistic creeds). The accent is all the more surprising in the context of a largely Christian narrative, given the traditional linkage of that faith with embodiment and "incarnation."[10] The downgrading or relative dismissal of the horizontal has clear repercussions with regard to "humanism" and the divine-human relationship. The conception of an "exclusive humanism" seems to leave ample room for a more open and nonexclusive type. Yet, despite an occasional acknowledgment of the possibility of nonexclusiveness, the point is not further developed or explored. Equally bypassed or sidelined is the possibility of a symbiosis of the divine, the human, and "nature"—a triadic structure requiring resolute openness on all sides. At one point, Taylor ponders the deleterious impact of a certain "non-religious anti-humanism" (associated mainly with Nietzsche and his followers). However, his own privileging of verticality conjures up the specter of a radically religious anti-humanism—a specter bound to be disturbing in the context of the current vogue of fundamentalist rhetoric.[11]

The Rhythm of Being

To some extent, the preceding paragraph can serve as a gateway to the work of Raimon Panikkar, the renowned Catalan-Indian philosopher and sage (who passed away on August 26, 2010). Among many other intellectual initiatives, Panikkar is known for his endorsement of a triadic structure of

Being—the so-called "cosmotheandric" conception—in which God (or the divine), human beings, and nature (or cosmos) are linked in indissoluble correlation or symbiosis. Seen from the angle of this conception, the radical separation or opposition between transcendence and an "immanent frame" seems far-fetched if not simply unintelligible. It is fairly clear that Panikkar could not or would not have written a book titled *A Secular Age* with a focus on immanentization. For one thing, the two terms of the title for him are synonymous—seeing that "age" is equivalent to the Latin *saeculum*. More importantly, the divine (or transcendent) in Panikkar's view cannot be divorced from the temporal (or "secular") without jeopardizing or destroying the intimate divine-human relation and thereby the aforementioned triadic structure. The distinctive and unconventional meaning of secularism or secularity is manifest in a number of his early writings which remain important in the present context. Thus, his book *Worship and Secular Man* (of 1973) put forward this provocative thesis: "Only worship can prevent secularization from becoming inhuman, and only secularization can save worship from being meaningless." To which he added this equally startling comment: "Now, what is emerging in our days, and what may be a 'hapax phenomenon,' a unique occurrence in the history of humankind, is—paradoxically—not secularism, but the sacred quality of secularism."[12]

Panikkar has never abandoned this provocative thesis; it still pervades powerfully his later writings, including *The Rhythm of Being*. As he notes in the preface to that book (written on Pentecost 2009), the original title of his Gifford Lectures was "The Dwelling of the Divine in the Contemporary World"—a phrase surely not far removed from the notion of sacred secularity. Although for various reasons the original title was changed, the "leading thread" of the book—he adds—"continues to be the same." What characterizes this "leading thread," despite textual revisions, is the idea of a radical "relationality" or "relativity" involving the three basic dimensions of reality: cosmos (nature), human beings, and God (or the divine)—where each of these dimensions is seen not as a static essence but as an active and dynamic participant in the ongoing transformation of reality or "Being." As Panikkar states, what he intends to convey in his book is a new sense of *creatio continua* in which each one of us, in St. Bonaventure's phrase, is a "co-creator." A crucial feature of the intended relationality is the close linkage between the "temporal" and the "eternal," or between time and Being. "Time," we read, "is not an accident to life, or to Being. . . . Each existence is *tempiternal* . . . and with this observation we have already reached our topic of the 'Rhythm of Being,' which is ever old and ever new." Instead of bogging down in irremediable ruptures and dichotomies, this rhythm proceeds in the modality of mediation (*utrum*, both, as well as) and thus in "the *advaitic* language."[13]

Along with other ruptures and dichotomies, *The Rhythm of Being* also refuses to accept the split between the "vertical" and "horizontal" dimensions of reality. In fact, despite its basically philosophical and meditative character, the book elaborates more explicitly on present-day social-political ills than does the Canadian political thinker. For Panikkar, dealing with the "rhythm of Being" cannot be a mode of escapism but involves a struggle about "the very meaning" of life and reality—a struggle which has to be attentive to all dimensions of reality, even the least appealing. "In a world of crisis, upheaval, and injustice," he asks, "can we disdainfully distance ourselves from the plight of the immense majority of the peoples of the world and dedicate ourselves to 'speculative' and/or 'theoretical' issues? Do we not thereby fall prey to the powers of the status quo?" In language which becomes ever more urgent and pleading, he continues:

> Can we really do "business as usual" in a world in which half of our fellow-beings suffer from man-made causes? Is our theory not already flawed by the praxis from which it proceeds? Are we not puppets in the hands of an oppressive system, lackeys to the powers that be, hypocrites who succumb to the allure and flattery of money, prestige, and honors? Is it not escapism to talk about the Trinity while the world falls to pieces and its people suffer all around us? . . . Have we seen the constant terror under which the "natives" and the "poor" are forced to live? What do we really know about the hundreds of thousands killed, starved, tortured, and *desaparecidos*, or about the millions of displaced and homeless people who have become the statistical commonplace of the mass media?[14]

For Panikkar, we cannot remain bystanders in the affairs of the world but have to become involved—without engaging in mindless or self-promoting activism. In a disjointed and disoriented world, what is needed above all is a genuine search for the truth of Being and the meaning of life—which basically involves a search for justice and the "good life" (or the goodness of life). "We are all co-responsible for the state of the world," Panikkar affirms. In the case of intellectuals or philosophers, this responsibility entails that they "ought to be incarnated in their own times and have an exemplary function," which in turn means the obligation "to search for truth (something that has saving power) and not to chase after irrelevant verities." Genuine search for the truth of life, however, proceeds from a lack or a perceived need which provides the compelling motivation for the quest: "Without this thirst for 'living waters,'" Panikkar writes, "there is no human life, no dynamism, no change. Thirst comes from lack of water." On this level, we are not dealing with epistemological, logical, or purely academic questions. Quest for life and its truth derives ultimately from "our existential thirst for the reign of justice," not from a passing interest or curiosity: "We are dealing with something that is more than an academic challenge. It is a spiritual endeavor to live the life that has been given us."[15]

The quest for life and its meaning, in Panikkar's presentation, is not simply a human initiative or an individual "project" (in Sartre's sense); nor is it an external destiny or a fate imposed from on high. The reason is that, in pursuit of the quest, the human seeker is steadily transformed, just as the goal of the search is constantly reformulated or refined. This is where Panikkar's "holistic" or nondualistic approach comes into play, his notion of a constantly evolving and interacting triadic structure. As he writes: "I would like to help awaken the dignity and responsibility of the individual by providing a holistic vision," and this can only happen if, in addition to our human freedom, we remain attentive to the *"freedom of Being* on which our human and cosmic dignity is grounded." From a holistic angle, the different elements of reality are not isolated fragments but interrelated partners in a symphony or symbiosis where they are neither identical nor divorced. "Each entity," Panikkar states, "is not just a part, but an image or icon of the Whole, as minimal and imperfect as that image may be." Holism thus stands opposed to the Cartesian dualistic (subject/object) epistemology, without necessarily subscribing to a dialectical synthesis where differences are "sublated" in a universal (Hegelian) system. Importantly, holism does not and cannot equal "totalism" or "totalitarianism" because no one can have a grasp or overview of the totality or the "Whole." "No single person," we read, "can reasonably claim to master a global point of departure. No individual exhausts the totality of possible approaches to the real." For Panikkar, the most adequate idiom in which to articulate such holism is the Indian language of Advaita Vedanta: "*Advaita* offers the adequate approach . . . [because it] entails a cordial order of intelligibility, of an *intellectus* that does not proceed dialectically." Different from rationalistic demonstration, the advaitic order is "intrinsically pluralistic."[16]

By overcoming Cartesian epistemology, advaitic holism inaugurates a close relation between human mind and reality, or (in different language) between "thinking" and "Being." In this relation, thought not only thinks *about* Being (as an external object), but Being penetrates thinking as its animating ground. As Panikkar states pointedly: "The underlying problem is that of thinking and Being." What is conjured up by this problem is the Vedantic conception of *atman-brahman* or else the Thomistic formula *anima quodammodo omnia*. Another, more general, idiom is that of ontology. In Panikkar's words: "The consecrated word for what we were pondering about the Whole is precisely 'Being'—and we shall not avoid this word any longer." At this point, the text offers a passage which is not only evocative of but directly congruent with Heideggerian formulations. "*Thinking 'thinks Being,'*" we read. "Being begets thinking; one might even risk saying: Being 'beings thinking'" (in line with Heidegger's phrase that Being "calls forth" thinking). "Thinking is such only," the passage continues, "if it is permeated by Being. Thinking is an activity of Being. Being thinks; otherwise thinking would be nothing." This does not mean, of course, that human thinking can ever exhaust Being—which would result in "totalism" or totalization. Rather, thinking and Being are responsive to each other in a rhythmic "complementarity" or a spirited embrace:

> The vision of the concrete in the Whole and the Whole in the concrete is, in fact, another way of saying that the relationship is rhythmic. Rhythm is not an "eternal return" in a static repetition . . . [but] rather the vital circle in the dance between the concrete and the Whole in which the concrete takes an ever-new form of the Whole.[17]

For human beings, participation in this dance means not only light-hearted entertainment but involvement in a transformative struggle to overcome selfishness or possessive self-centeredness. Panikkar speaks in this context of a "purification of the heart," which is needed in order to join the dance. He quotes at this point the words of Hugo of Saint-Victor: "The way to ascend to God is to descend into oneself"; and also the parallel statement by Richard of Saint-Victor: "Let man ascend through himself above himself." What is involved here is not merely an epistemic principle, nor a purely deontological duty, but "an ontological requirement." As Panikkar stresses, the issue here is neither esoteric nor a private whim but simply this: that we shall not discover our real situation, collectively as well as individually, "if our hearts are not pure, if our lives are not in harmony within ourselves, with our surroundings, and ultimately with the universe [Being] at large." The text here adds a passage that can serve as the passkey to Panikkar's entire vision: "Only when the heart is pure are we in harmony with the real, in tune with reality, able to hear its voice, detect its dynamism, and truly 'speak' its truth, having become adequate to the movement of Being, the Rhythm of Being." The passage refers to the Chinese *Chung Yung* (in Ezra Pound's translation), saying: "Only the most absolute sincerity under heaven can effect any change," and adds: "The spiritual masters of every age agree that only when the waters of our spirit are tranquil can they reflect reality without deforming it."[18]

What becomes clear in this context is that some of Panikkar's key notions—like the "cosmotheandric" vision or "sacred secularity"—are not simply neutral-descriptive devices but are imbued with a dynamic, transformative potency. As one should note, however—and this is crucial—his notions do not reflect a bland optimism or trust in a "better future" but are based on "hope," which is a hope "of the invisible," a hope for a promised possibility. With regard to "sacred secularity," this possibility is not an empty pipe dream but is supported by a novel phenomenon (a *novum*) in our time: "This *novum* does not take refuge in the highest by neglecting the lowest; it does not make a separation by favoring the spiritual and ignoring the material; it does not search out eternity at the expense of temporality." Differently phrased: the *novum* consists in a growing attentiveness to holism in lieu of the customary polarities (of *this* world and the *other* world, the inner and the outer, the secular and the divine). A still further way to express the *novum* is the growing awareness of the "Rhythm of Being" and the growing willingness to participate in that rhythm. What is becoming manifest, we read, is that "we all participate in Rhythm," and that "Rhythm is another name for Being and Being is Trinity." The last formulation refers again to the triadic or "cosmotheandric" structure of reality. For, Panikkar states, "rhythm is intrinsically connected with any activity of the gods, men, and nature." In more traditional language, one might say that rhythm is "the cosmotheandric order of the universe, the *perichoresis* (*circuminsessio*, mutual in-dwelling) of the radical Trinity."[19]

As in the case of Taylor's *A Secular Age*, it cannot be my aim here to submit Panikkar's entire volume to reflective review and scrutiny. A few additional points must suffice. One point concerns the traditional conception of monotheism. The notion of *perichoresis*—coupled with the accent on the "meta-transcendental" status of Being—does not seem to accord well with monotheistic "transcendence." In fact, Panikkar's text subjects the conception to strong critique. As he writes at one point: "I suspect that the days of unqualified theisms are not going to be bright." What troubles Panikkar, apart from philosophical considerations, is the implicit connection of monotheism with a heteronomous command structure ("God, King, President, Police"). "The titles of King and Lord," we read, "fit the monotheistic God quite well, and conversely, the human king could easily be the representative of God, and his retinue a copy of the heavenly hierarchies." This is the gist of "political theology" (so-called). To be sure, traditional hierarchies no longer prevail—despite recurrent attempts at constructing "theocracies." What is required in the context of modern democracy is a radical rethinking of the monotheistic command structure. In Panikkar's words: "Regardless of certain forms of fundamentalism, both Christianity and Judaism clearly show that human freedom and love of neighbor belong to the *kernel* of their message." This means that any "revealed" monotheism must ultimately acknowledge its intrinsic reference to its "human reception" (and hence to *circuminsessio*). Differently phrased: Divine revelation "has to fall on human grounds in order to be a belief for humans." This belief is "a human experience, humanly interpreted, and humanly received into the collective consciousness of a culture at a given time." Summarizing his view, Panikkar writes:

> My position . . . is neither naively iconoclastic nor satisfied with a reformed monotheism. It recognizes the valid insight of belief in God, but at the same time it acknowledges that God is not the only symbol for that third dimension we call the Divine, and it attempts to deepen the human experience of the Divine by formulating it more convincingly for our times.[20]

In a central chapter of the book, titled "The Dwelling of the Divine" (capturing the originally intended title of the Gifford Lectures), Panikkar returns to the central meaning of the triadic structure understood as mutual in-dwelling. As he reaffirms, one-sided theisms "no longer seem to be able to satisfy the most profound urges of the contemporary sensibilities." What is coming into view instead is *perichoresis* seen as radical relationality where "everything is permeated by everything else." Seen from this angle, "man is 'more' than just an individual being, the Divine 'different' from a Supreme Lord, and the world 'other' than raw material to be plundered for utility or profit." This view can be grasped in the language neither of transcendence nor that of immanence, because "we cannot even think" one without the other. Thus, where does the Divine dwell? "I would say," Panikkar states, "that the space of man is in God in much the same way as the space of God is in man." From this perspective, man and God are not two separable, independent substances: "There is no real *two* encompassing man and God . . . , but they are not *one* either. Man and God are neither *one* nor *two*." This, again, is the language of "advaitic intuition" (perhaps of Heideggerian *Unterschied*). Advaita, we are told here, does not simply mean "monism," but rather "the overcoming of dualistic dialectics by means of introducing love [or wisdom] at the ultimate level of reality." Regarding the trinitarian structure, Panikkar takes pains to broaden the conception beyond traditional Christian theology. Both "esoteric Judaism and esoteric Islam," he notes, are familiar with the threefold structure of the Divine. Thus, Philo of Alexandria interpreted the vision of Abraham and his three "visitors" in a trinitarian fashion. The Muslim mystic Ibn Arabi was even more explicit when he wrote: "My beloved is three / —three yet only one; / many things appear as three / which are no more than one." And the Chinese Taoist Yang Hsiung explained the "great mystery" as constituting simultaneously "the way of Heaven, the way of Earth, and the way of Man."[21]

Toward the end of his book, Panikkar returns to the relation of meditation and praxis, of thinking and doing in a transformative process. As he writes: "The task of transforming the cosmos is not achieved by a merely passive attitude nor by sheer activism." What is needed is a "synergy" in which human beings are seen neither as designing engineers nor as victims: "The world does not 'go' independently from us. We are also active factors in the destiny of the cosmos. Otherwise, discourse about the dignity of man, his 'divinization' or divine character is an illusion." Seen from an advaitic angle, "man" is a "microcosmos" and even a "microtheos." Hence, human participation in the rhythm of the cosmos means "a sharing in the divine dimension" or what is sometimes called "salvation history." Participation in this dynamism is indeed a striving for a "better world"—but a striving where the latter is "neither the dream of an earthly paradise nor [a retreat into] the inner self alone," but rather a struggle for "a world with less hatred and more love, with less violence and more justice." For Panikkar, this struggle is urgent because the situation of our world today is "tragic" and "serious enough to call for radical measures." Ultimately, the struggle involves a quest for the "meaning of Life," which will never be found through selfish exploits or violent conquest, but only "in reaching that fullness of Life to which [advaitic] contemplation is the way." As Panikkar finally pleads: "Plenitude, happiness, creativity, freedom, well-being, achievement etc. should not be given up but, on the contrary, should be enhanced by this transformative passage" from man-made history to a triadic redemptive story.[22]

Concluding Comments

The passage just cited highlights an important difference between Taylor and Panikkar. Basically, *The Rhythm of Being* is an affirmation and celebration of "life" in its deeper advaitic meaning. Panikkar uses as equivalents the terms "plenitude, happiness, creativity, freedom, well-being"; another customary term is "flourishing" (often used to translate Aristotle's *eudaimonia*). At another point, he introduces the word "life" "at the level of Being, as a human experience of the Whole"; the term here means "not only *anima*, animal life, but *physis, natura, prakriti*" referring to "reality as a Whole." On this issue, *A Secular Age* appears astonishingly (and unduly) dismissive. As Taylor notes in his introduction, in modernity "we have moved from a world in which the place of fullness was understood as unproblematically outside or 'beyond' human life, to a conflicted age in which this construal is challenged by others which place it . . . 'within' human life." For Taylor (as mentioned before), the basic question raised by the modern secular age is "whether people [still] recognize something beyond or transcendent to their lives," that is, whether their highest aim is "serving a good which is beyond, in the sense of independent of human flourishing" or involving "something other than human flourishing?" The truly believing or devout person is said to be marked by readiness "to make a profound inner break with the goals of flourishing in their own case"; unwillingness to do so is claimed to be the hallmark of "self-sufficient humanism." In sum: "A secular age is one in which the eclipse of all goals beyond human flourishing becomes conceivable."[23]

Taylor's comments here are puzzling—and also disturbing. They are disturbing in a time when many, presumably religious, people are ready to throw away their lives in the hope of gaining quick access to the "beyond." They are puzzling by jeopardizing the very meaning of faith. For most believers, salvation (or *moksha*) signifies precisely the highest level of flourishing and the ultimate fulfillment of life. What, then, does it mean for believers to seek something "outside or 'beyond' human life," or something "transcendent to their lives"? Commonly, the antithesis of life is said to be death. Is God (the monotheistic God) then a God of death or of the dead?

Clearly, this cannot be the case if we listen to Isaiah's words: "The dead shall live, their bodies shall rise" (Isaiah 26:19). It becomes even less plausible if we recall Jesus's provocative saying: "Follow me, and leave the dead to bury their dead" (Matthew 8:22), or his admonition that "the Father raises the dead and gives them life" (John 5:21). As it happens, Taylor himself waivers on this point and has to resort to ambivalent language. "There remains a fundamental tension in Christianity," he writes. "Flourishing is good, nevertheless seeking it is not our ultimate goal. But even when we renounce it, we re-affirm it." And he adds: "The injunction 'Thy will be done' is not equivalent to 'Let humans flourish,' even though we know that God wills human flourishing."[24]

Rather than pursuing the contrast between the two thinkers, however, I want to emphasize here a commonality. While differing in many ways, neither Taylor nor Panikkar shows sympathy for theocracy or for any kind of religious triumphalism. Being turned off by the megalomania and massive power plays of our world, both thinkers are sensitive to new modes of religiosity—quite outside impressive spectacles and miraculous events. As it seems to me, one of the distinctive features of our age is not so much the "death of God" or the lack of faith, but rather the withdrawal and sheltering of the divine in the recessed, inconspicuous phenomena of ordinary life. The Indian novelist Arundhati Roy has caught this aspect in her book *The God of Small Things*. Inspired by the Indian text, I tried to capture the sense of (what I called) "small wonder" in one of my earlier writings. Here are some lines:

> For too long, I fear, the divine has been usurped and co-opted by powerful elites for their own purposes. . . . For too long in human history the divine has been nailed to the cross of worldly power. However, in recent times, there are signs that the old alliance may be ending and that religious faith may begin to liberate itself from the chains of worldly manipulation. Exiting from the palaces and mansions of the powerful, faith—joined by philosophical wisdom—is beginning to take shelter in inconspicuous smallness, in those recesses of ordinary life unavailable to co-optation.[25]

The change in religious sensibility is vividly displayed in modern art, especially in modern and contemporary painting. As we know, in medieval art the presence of the divine or the sacred was expressed symbolically by a golden background and the haloes surrounding sacred figures. Modern art cannot honestly, or without caricature, imitate or replicate this mode of expression. This does not mean that the sense of sacredness has been lost or abandoned. As it seems to me, that sense resurfaces in less obvious, more subdued ways, for example, in the miniature paintings of Paul Klee or else in a still life by Paul Cézanne. Viewed from this angle, modern secularism has a recessed meaning which is actually the very reverse of the popular "secularization thesis" (meaning the triumph of this-worldliness). The French philosopher Maurice Merleau-Ponty—a strong admirer of Cézanne—had a phrase for it, "the invisible of the visible." Seen against this background, the relation between the two books reviewed here—*A Secular Age* and *The Rhythm of Being*—acquires a new meaning. Perhaps, one might conjecture, the "secular age," as portrayed by Taylor, functioned and functions as wholesome conduit, a clearing agent, to guide a more mature and sober humanity to the appreciation of the "rhythm of Being." If this is so (at least in approximation), then it may be propitious to remember Hölderlin's lines: "But where there is danger, a saving grace also grows."[26]

5

"MAN AGAINST THE STATE"

Self-Interest and Civil Resistance

Let your life be a counter-friction to stop the machine.

—Henry David Thoreau

The opening part of *Thus Spoke Zarathustra* contains these stark lines: "State is the name of the coldest of all cold monsters. Coldly it tells lies too; and this lie crawls out of its mouth: I, the state, am the people." These lines resonate strongly with contemporary ears, not only in totalitarian autocracies but in (so-called) democracies as well. Everywhere people are confronted with mammoth corruption and vile deceptions perpetrated by "states." Nietzsche calls the state the coldest monster because it is devoid of human sensibility and, in fact, has turned into a huge technical artifact or machine. In Western thought, Thomas Hobbes was the first to call the state an "artificial body"; but at his time, this artifact was still embodied in a human sovereign. In the meantime, the sovereign has been replaced or supplemented by an immense bureaucratic apparatus, an apparatus inhabited by "specialists without spirit" and wedded solely to digital calculation and electronic surveillance. More importantly, under the aegis of this apparatus, life and death are increasingly mechanized, with military valor being replaced by automated killing machines. "Indeed," Zarathustra exclaims, "a hellish artifice was invented here, a horse of death, clattering in the finery of divine honors." If these developments continue, the prospects for human life and freedom are dismal: "Verily, this sign [of the state] signifies the will to death. It beckons to the preachers of death."[1]

The state castigated in Nietzsche's text is far removed from the older conception of a political community or "polis," a term designating a shared public life sustained by ethical bonds and by (what Aristotle called) a "watery kind of friendship." Nietzsche is not dismissive of this older notion. In fact, he puts into Zarathustra's mouth these memorable lines: "It was creators who created peoples and hung a faith and a love over them: thus they served life." And with creative life comes freedom: "A free life is still free for great souls . . . Only where the 'state' ends, there begins the human being who is not superfluous." As one should note here, a "free life" is not intrinsically opposed to a freely shared solidarity, that is, to a life shared with friends in whom (as Nietzsche says) "the world stands completed, a bowl of goodness."[2] The aim of the present essay is to show the compatibility between a properly conceived freedom and a properly conceived solidarity, more precisely between an unselfish or self-transcending freedom and an uncoercive, future-oriented public community. It must be recognized, however, that this relationship is always tensional and fraught with profound hazards—hazards which can arise from either side or from both, leading to a rupture of the ethical social bond. Despotism and totalizing autocracy provoke a rupture "from above," while radical individualism and violent rebellion tear the social fabric "from below."

In modern Western thought, the antithetical formula of "man versus the state" is associated chiefly with a certain type of liberalism or "libertarianism" promoted by Herbert Spencer and his followers. In the following, I discuss in a first step this formula, sometimes called "social Darwinism," which has exerted great influence in the West in recent times. In a second step, I turn to more nuanced and ethically sensitive formulations of the "freedom-solidarity" conundrum advanced by Thoreau, Gandhi, and Albert Camus. By way of conclusion I offer some additional examples of the freedom-solidarity nexus by turning to the trial of Socrates and the ethically inspired resistance movement against the Nazi regime in Germany.

Herbert Spencer and Social Darwinism

Tensions and internal conflicts are endemic to most societies and political regimes. As history teaches, societies East and West have always been periodically in the throes of domestic upheavals and rebellions. However, in the past such rebellions have typically originated in perceived social and political ills and are motivated by the goal of establishing a more just or acceptable regime (from the angle of the insurgents). One of the strikingly novel features in Western modernity is that domestic challenges are sometimes directed against regimes as such, that is, against the very notion of a shared public order. In large measure, this feature is associated with modern liberalism (sometimes shading over into anarchism), a doctrine anchored in the primacy of individual self-interest. Still, even in the context of modern liberalism, a radical antisocial or "anti-state" animus developed only slowly. Thus, although assuming a radically individualistic and asocial "state of nature," Hobbes maintained firmly that reason and internalized moral codes would eventually lead people to construct a stable regime. Likewise, while departing from a similar (though nearly peaceful) state of nature, John Locke's liberal public order inserted individual rights squarely into the framework of an established social community (whose unraveling was treated as a rare exception). It was only in the nineteenth century, under the impact of positivism and evolutionism, that the liberal creed became virulent, in the sense of normalizing the Hobbesian state of nature.

Basically, the nineteenth century witnessed a confluence of intellectual tendencies, many of which conspired to drive the notion of a shared normative order underground. One was the emergence of the discipline of "sociology," inaugurated by Auguste Comte, with its focus on empirical description in opposition to the "metaphysical" assumptions of the earlier age of the Enlightenment. Another feature, located in the ethical domain, was the rise to prominence of "utilitarianism," a quasi-psychological doctrine initiated by Jeremy Bentham, which located normative standards not in abstract "laws of nature" but in the empirical calculus of pleasure and pain. A third trend gathering momentum throughout the century was biological evolutionism, which reached its most mature expression in the work of Charles Darwin. In an instructive and exemplary fashion, the three cited trends converged and reached an (unstable) synthesis in the writings of Herbert Spencer (1820–1903), a prominent sociologist and social philosopher deeply influenced by Comtean positivism, utilitarian teachings, and later in life by Darwin's *On the Origin of Species* (first published in 1859). Because of this intellectual indebtedness, Spencer is sometimes regarded as a purely derivative thinker—which is not entirely fair. Thus, while honoring Comte, he did not embrace his historical "stage theory," favoring a more flexible evolutionism. With regard to utilitarianism, he sought to improve the dominant rigid empiricism by preferring a more "rational" or enlightened version (which even made room for "natural rights" dismissed by Jeremy Bentham). His relation to Darwin was complex and by no means reducible to a simple transfer of ideas from biology to sociology.[3]

During his lifetime, Spencer's writings were received widely and mostly favorably; however, none of his other texts could match the impact, both then and later, achieved by his book published in 1884 under the title *The Man versus the State*. The book is a collection of essays dealing with a variety of topics; however, the central thrust of the text is a virulent polemical attack on what Spencer called the "new Toryism"—a code word for the shift of British liberalism in the direction of an interventionist and paternalistic "statism" (typical of old-style Tory conservatism). In eloquent and stirring language, the book pits against each other a military and "militant" regime associated with Toryism/conservatism and a commercial or "industrial" social order promoted by genuine liberalism; while, in the former, social bonds are hierarchical and compulsory, in the second case they are voluntary and minimal (in accordance with laissez-faire principles of individual freedom and private property). Contemporary readers of the text, confronted with the "monstrosity" of state bureaucracies, are likely to appreciate Spencer's polemic—especially when the latter is extended to a scathing critique of state-sponsored colonial or imperial expansions across the globe. As it happens, however, this appreciation is bound to diminish or be muted by Spencer's political naïveté, his inability or unwillingness to ponder the effects of the ongoing replacement of "industrialism" by new capitalist hierarchies whose leaders were eager to step into the vacated place of public institutions. The disaffection is deepened by Spencer's relentless attacks on public education, unionism, and social welfare legislation seeking to provide a buffer against the new forms of economic domination.

In many ways, *The Man versus the State* follows the lead of earlier liberal thinkers—but with a significant twist. Together with Hobbes and Locke, the text starts from the assumption of individual liberty in a pristine "natural" condition, stating: "There are no phenomena which a society presents but what have their origins in the phenomena of individual life, which again have their roots in vital phenomena at large." By contrast to the opinion of his predecessors, however, Spencer does not find original social life beset with sufficient inconveniences so as to prompt members to leave that condition in favor of a mutual engagement leading to the formation of a public regime. As if guided by natural instinct, participants in society—on Spencer's account—pursue their individual self-interest while respecting definite limits and, as good merchants or businessmen, abide by commercial contracts negotiated for their mutual benefit. In his words: "Though mere love of companionship prompts primitive men to live in groups, yet the chief prompter is experience of the advantages to be derived from cooperation." On what condition, he asks, can such cooperation arise? "Evidently only on condition that those who join their efforts severally gain by doing so." If this expectation is frustrated or if mutuality is disrupted, there will be "a reversion to that rudest condition in which each man makes everything for himself. Hence, the possibility of cooperation depends on the fulfillment of [commercial] contract, tacit or overt." Drawing the conclusion from these comments, the text insists that only industry and, in fact, a "vast elaborate industrial organization" can insure social progress: "For in proportion as contracts are unhindered and the performance of them certain, the growth is great and the social life active."[4]

As one should note, the maintenance of commercial engagements is entrusted here entirely to the "natural" disposition of individuals, quite outside the functioning of public institutions and also outside any civic education (nurturing moral and civic habits among individuals and groups). It is in this sense that "man" (in "man versus the state") is originally in possession of "natural rights," including the right of individual liberty and the secure enjoyment of private property. If they had taken this stark opposition more seriously, Spencer argues, Bentham's utilitarian disciples might have been led "to treat less cavalierly the doctrine of natural rights." Far from having anything to do with public institutions or rules, rights for Spencer originate simply in the spontaneous "mutual limitation of activities" among people, as demonstrated by "the few peaceful tribes which have either nominal governments or none at all." Having been established "more or less clearly before government arises," rights "become obscured as government develops." Spencer, to be sure, is not unaware that commercial agreements are vulnerable to breach and need to be somehow maintained or guaranteed. Hence, the central maxim of his text is "that contracts shall be free and fulfillment of them enforced." However, enforcement takes the form chiefly of spontaneous self-limitation (reducing the role of government to that of a "night watchman" of property). "There must be, in the first place," he writes, "few restrictions on man's liberties to make agreements with one another, and there must be, in the second place, an enforcement of the agreements which they do make." But, preferably, these checks are "those only which result from mutual limitation," and consequently "there can be no resulting check to the contracts they voluntarily make."[5]

In addition to Comtean and utilitarian leanings, Spencer (as stated before) was also greatly attracted to Darwin's work and to biological evolutionism more generally. This attraction has prompted many critics to present him as a proponent of "social Darwinism" (a label meaning the transfer of the principle of natural-biological selection to social relations).[6] Used as a summary verdict, the portrayal seems exaggerated, given Spencer's preference for "synthesizing" many views (including the utilitarian maxim of "the greatest good for the greatest number"). Still it is hard to deny certain "social Darwinist" features in his work. Thus, after having read Darwin's *Origin of Species*, he is reported to have coined the phrase "survival of the fittest," an expression which soon became a catchphrase in discussions of both biological and social evolution. That Spencer himself was ready to transfer aspects of the "survival" motto to the social and political domain is evident from his *The Man versus the State*. As we read there, the "vital principle" of individual and social life, and indeed the vital principle of "social progress," is maintained if each individual is "left secure in person and possessions to satisfy his wants with its proceeds." Despite its broad generality, the concrete application of this principle quickly reveals stark social differences, deriving from the diversity of individual aptitudes and energies. The principle, Spencer adds, is a guarantee of progress "inasmuch as, under given conditions, the individuals of most worth will prosper and multiply more than those of less worth."

Seen in this light, the idea of "utility," properly understood, enjoins "the maintenance of individual rights" despite different outcomes. Any attempt to interfere with this principle—especially by "meddling legislation"—is "a proposal to improve life by breaking down the fundamental conditions to life."[7] Whatever Spencer's own leanings may have been, reception of his work soon inspired (rightly or wrongly) a broad movement of "social Darwinism" throughout the world. In America, the undisputed leader of the movement was William Graham Sumner (1840–1910), a sociologist and social theorist who combined Spencer's teachings with neo-classical ideas of free enterprise, a combination made plausible by the rapid rise of unfettered capitalism in America at that time. In a highly influential pamphlet published in 1883 under the title *What Social Classes Owe to Each Other*, Sumner insisted that social classes owe each other precisely nothing, relying for this conclusion on a version of the "survival of the fittest" motto. In a stark swipe at any form of socialism, Sumner excoriated all attempts to alleviate or uplift the lot of disadvantaged people or classes as an assault on social progress and advancement; given their essential role as social pioneers, business people and economic enterprises were to be left as free as possible from taxes and public regulations.

From England and America, Spencerian and social Darwinist ideas migrated to many other places, often greatly revising or modifying their initial emphases (sometimes becoming fused with doctrines of racial eugenics).[8] The strongest and most lasting impact of *The Man versus the State*, however, was exerted on the field of neo-classical economics, and especially on the so-called "Austrian School" of economics, wedded to the celebration of the untrammeled pursuit of private and corporate profit. As formulated by one of the leaders of the school, the basic principle of capitalism is public nonintervention in the market (laissez-faire), especially noninterference in status differences: "The inequality of incomes and wealth is an inherent characteristic of the market economy. Its elimination would totally destroy the [capitalist] market economy."[9]

Civil Disobedience and Dissent

Strictly construed, Spencer's formula of "man versus the state" erects a gulf between individuals and governments; in a slight modification, social Darwinism stresses the gulf between individual advancement and social or public arrangements hampering the pursuit of self-interest. In each case, the guiding assumption is that of a "zero sum" game, that is, of a radical antithesis of interests where neither side owes anything to the other. What is (at least tendentially) expunged in this game is the notion of shared social bonds, of a civic community circumscribing naked self-interest. To be sure, bonds of this kind do not by themselves eliminate the possibility of profound tensions and even conflicts in society. The cause of such conflicts is typically the failure of some agents to live up to the ethical obligations implicit in social life. On the part of individuals (or groups of individuals), remonstrations or uprisings typically take the character of "civil disobedience" or conscientious "resistance" to perceived public corruption or repression. What is important to note here is the stark difference between social Darwinism and the latter kind of disobedience: whereas in the former case anti-public conduct is rooted in the pursuit of private self-interest, in the case of disobedience or conscientious resistance the motive is to enhance or restore public well-being and justice in society. A particularly inspiring text along these lines was penned by the New England writer Henry David Thoreau in his essay "Resistance to Civil Government" (1849), later renamed "Essay on Civil Disobedience."

The opening lines of the essay seem to place Thoreau squarely on the side of Spencer and other laissez-faire liberals of the time. "I heartily accept the motto," he states, "that 'government is best which governs least';

and I should like to see it acted up to more rapidly and systematically."
Government, he adds, is "best but an expedient, but most governments are
usually, and all governments are sometimes, inexpedient." Even in democracies, where people presumably choose their leaders, government is "equally
liable to be abused and perverted before the people can act through it." Take
the example of the American government, an institution with a venerable
tradition but which "each instant is losing some of its integrity." Although
formally democratic, it has turned into a vast bureaucracy, a "complicated
machinery" imposing itself on the people; it is "a sort of wooden gun to
the people themselves." Echoing some of Spencer's more captivating lines,
Thoreau exclaims: "This government never of itself furthered any enterprise.
It does not keep the country free. It does not settle the West. It does not
educate. The character inherent in the American people has done all that
has been accomplished." The upshot of these comments is that government
is more a burden than a benefactor of the people or an engine of progress:
"Government is an expedient by which men would fain succeed in letting
one another alone; and . . . when it is most expedient, the governed are
most let alone by it."[10]

While seemingly toeing a radical libertarian line, Thoreau's essay at
this point adds a twist which points in a completely different direction.
"But to speak practically and as a citizen," he states, "unlike those who call
themselves 'no-government' men, I ask for, not at once no government,
but *at once* a better government. Let every man make known what kind of
government would command his respect, and that will be one step toward
obtaining it." With these words, Thoreau introduces an ethical standard
which Spencer and radical liberals sidestep: the standard of social justice
discerned by human conscience. "Can there not be a government," he asks,
"in which majorities do not virtually decide right and wrong [relying on
their power alone] but conscience?" A government where majorities decide
or determine "only those questions to which the rule of expediency [not
rightness] is applicable?" This question leads to the role of citizens in a public
regime. Should citizens simply "resign their conscience" to the government?
But then, "why has every man a conscience?" "I think," Thoreau insists,
"that we should be men [human beings] first, and subjects afterwards." This
principle also applies to business enterprises. For, "it is truly enough said that
a corporation has no conscience; but a corporation of conscientious men is
a corporation *with* a conscience." In every instance, the guiding yardstick
must be that "it is not desirable to cultivate a respect for the [positive] law
so much as for the right" or just law. When this rule is reversed, human

beings become lackeys of government and possibly "agents of injustice." In that case, Thoreau adds with some sarcasm, "you may see a file of soldiers, colonel, captain, corporal, privates, powder-monkeys and all, marching in admirable order over hill and dale to the wars, against their wills, ay, against their common sense and consciences."[11]

In eloquent language, Thoreau's essay anticipates and condemns the steady transformation of governments into soulless machines, into grotesque bureaucratic apparatuses of control. People who follow such governments in blind obedience, he asks, "what are they?" Are they "men at all, or rather small movable forts and magazines, at the service of some unscrupulous man in power?" Unfortunately, even in democracies, such blind submission is widespread: "The mass of men serves the state thus, not as men mainly, but as machines, with their bodies. They are the standing army, and the militia, jailers, constables, *posse comitatus*." In such circumstances, there is in most cases "no free exercise whatever of judgment or of the moral sense," since "they put themselves on a level with wood and earth and stones—and perhaps wooden men [or else automata] can be manufactured that will serve the purpose as well." According to Thoreau, even people who are "commonly esteemed good citizens" often prefer to act in conformity with mechanical rules rather than raise their voice in alarm or opposition. In most societies, exceptions to this conduct are rare—and they are usually made to pay for their nonconformism. In Thoreau's words: "A very few—as heroes, patriots, martyrs, reformers in the great sense, and *men*—serve the state with their consciences also, and so resist it for the most part." But he adds (in a warning to all conscientious objectors, civil resisters, and whistleblowers): "And they are commonly treated as enemies by it."[12]

Thoreau did not only write about the consequences of resistance; he took some upon himself. For some six years he refused to pay a poll tax and he was put into prison for a while. But he did not seek to evade the penalty. As he states in his essay: "Under a government which imprisons any unjustly, the true place for a just man is also a prison." His refusal to pay taxes was meant as a protest against slavery and against the Mexican-American War, both of which he considered profoundly unjust. (One can safely guess what he would have done at the time of the Vietnam and Iraq wars.) The important point to consider is that his act of resistance was prompted not by any desire for personal gain, profit, or influence, but for ethical reasons which sometimes require suffering or sacrifice. If an injustice is of such a nature, he writes, "that it requires you to be the agent of injustice to another, then, I say, break the law. Let your life be a counter-friction to stop the machine." His sentiments toward his own government prior to the abolition of slavery were radical—and still upset some American readers. "How does it become a man to behave toward this American government today?" he asks. "I answer, that he cannot without disgrace be associated with it. I cannot for an instant recognize that political organization as *my* government which is the *slave's* government also" (or which enslaves other people). As he adds, again somewhat provocatively: "Action from principle, the perception and performance of right, changes things and relations; it is essentially revolutionary and does not consist wholly with anything which was." What remains crucial here is that change is not pursued for its own sake but for the sake of social and public improvement: "I please myself with imagining a state at last which can afford to be just to all men, and to treat the individual with respect as a neighbor."[13]

Thoreau's text was favorably received by many audiences, both in the West and in non-Western countries. The most important non-Western reader was Mohandas Gandhi, who considered the text as a welcome supportive inspiration for his own endeavors. To be sure, although a lifelong admirer of Thoreau (as well as John Ruskin and Tolstoy), Gandhi modified the former's approach in many ways, mainly by shifting the accent from individual or solitary initiatives to the collective concerns of broader social movements (without neglecting, of course, the role of individual conscience). As is well known, the idea of civil and social resistance first preoccupied Gandhi during his struggle against apartheid in South Africa, a struggle which later morphed into the movement for national independence from British rule in India. Despite the vastly changed location of resistance—from Walden Pond to India—the spirit or guiding animus of the struggle remained largely the same: the pursuit of justice and social-political improvement. At no point in his life was Gandhi motivated by the desire for wealth, influence, or public power; even at the time when independence was within reach, he refused to seek a governmental position. When initiating the resistance in South Africa, Gandhi tellingly gave to his movement the name *satyagraha*, a term which literally means "truth doing," that is, active pursuit of truth and justice. It has also been translated as "truth-force," "soul-force," or "love-force." As Erik Erikson has pointed out, in his famous study *Gandhi's Truth*, it was precisely the ethical and spiritual motivation which gave to Gandhi's independence struggle its special quality, distinguishing it from purely political rebellions. If the stress is placed only on struggle for power, he said, one misses "the spiritual origin of nonviolent courage in Gandhi's truth."[14]

Erikson's comment points to an important aspect of Gandhian truth-performance or justice-seeking: its reliance on nonviolence. There can be little doubt that, for Gandhi, the guiding principle of social struggle and resistance was nonviolent action (*ahimsa*) and that, in his view, *satyagraha* and *ahimsa* were intimately linked. As he stated in one of his writings on the topic: "In the application of *satyagraha*, I discovered in the earliest stages that pursuit of truth did not admit of violence being inflicted on one's opponent, but that he must be weaned from error by patience and sympathy."[15] The main point here is that for Gandhi—as for Socrates and Jesus before him—it is better to suffer injustice than to impose injustice on others. In Erikson's interpretation, Gandhian truth-performance was governed by "the readiness to get hurt and yet not to hurt"; if there was a guiding "dogma" in this approach, it was the maxim that "the only test of truth or justice is action based on the refusal to do harm." This maxim—importantly—was not only a cognitive or theoretical formula but achieved its cogency only by being "put to work" in concrete circumstances. Gandhi's enactment of the maxim was evident throughout his life, in his willingness to accept suffering in the form of fasting, imprisonment, abuse, and ultimately death—a willingness guided by the desire to appeal to the conscience and better ethical qualities of opponents. Here is another quotation from Gandhi's work: "Suffering is the law of human beings, war is the law of the jungle. But suffering is infinitely more powerful than the law of the jungle for converting the opponent and opening his ears, which are otherwise shut to the voice of reason."[16]

In recent times, this connection of justice and nonviolence has tended to be widely sidelined or entirely thrown to the winds—with predictable results. Totally neglecting both Thoreau's and Gandhi's teachings, some recent so-called "rebellions" have preferred to indulge in orgies of violence and acts of barbarism, always eagerly employing mayhem not as a last but as the first resort. But the consequences cannot be in doubt. For how can a rebellion pursued with brutal and destructive means lead to anything other than a brutal and destructive regime? How can a movement willing to repress and slaughter opponents lead to anything other than a repressive machine slaughtering dissenters? Against the engines of violence spiraling out of control, it is important and timely to invoke the teachings not only of Thoreau and Gandhi but also of the French writer Albert Camus, whose famous book *The Rebel* (1951) is a celebration of life and an antidote to the cult of death and destruction.

Camus's book takes its point of departure from the late-modern condition of "nihilism," the progressive self-devaluation of traditional values.

In the face of this situation, that is, the perceived lack of a preordained meaning of things, the nihilist concludes that everything is permitted, including killing and murder. *The Rebel* is in the first instance a rebellion against this conclusion. As Camus shows, the encounter of the nihilist with the perceived meaninglessness of the world—what he calls the "absurdist" encounter—is based on an act of judgment, an act which presupposes the self-affirmation of the judging agent and hence an affirmation of life. "It is obvious," he argues, "that absurdism [the absurdist encounter] hereby admits that human life is the only necessary good since it is precisely life that makes this encounter possible. To say [as the nihilist does] that life is absurd, the conscience must be alive." However, the affirmation of life cannot stop at the banishing of suicide or self-annihilation but carries a broader significance. "From the moment," the text continues, "that life is recognized as good, it becomes good for all men. Murder cannot be made coherent when suicide is not considered coherent." For Camus, proceeding on the premise of nihilism, there can be no half-measures: "Absurdist reasoning cannot defend the continued existence of the spokesman and, simultaneously, accept the sacrifice of others' lives. The moment we recognize the impossibility of absolute negation—and merely to be alive is to recognize this—the very first thing that cannot be denied is the right of others to live."[17]

As can be seen, rebellion in Camus's treatment is not a purely individualistic or self-centered venture but has broader social implications: the freedom of the rebel relies on a solidarity with other human beings and, in fact, with humanity. In his words: "Rebellion, contrary to current opinion, questions the very idea of the [isolated] individual. If the individual, in fact, accepts death and happens to die as a consequence of his act of rebellion, he demonstrates by doing so that he is willing to sacrifice himself for the sake of a common good which he considers more important than his own destiny." In going beyond his own self-interest or selfish desires, the rebel affirms and upholds an ethical order of rightness and justice which reveals a deeper human bond. Thus, in contrast to Spencerian libertarians, rebellion for Camus is not "an egoistic act" but a conduct gaining its sense or significance from its insertion into a social community. Basically, even in challenging existing rules, the rebel does so in order to improve them, bending them in the direction of social justice. As Camus adds, in a stark modification of the traditional Cartesian formula: "In our daily trials, rebellion plays the same role as does the '*cogito*' in the realm of thought: it is the first piece of evidence. But this evidence lures the individual from his solitude. It founds its first value on the whole human race: I rebel—therefore we are."[18]

Long before the terms became common currency, Camus's book speaks of violent "state terrorism" and the equally violent counterterror—either irrational or ideologically sophisticated—unleashed by insurgents. For him, the two sides of terror feed and have always fed on each other. "All modern [violent] revolutions," *The Rebel* states, "have ended in a reinforcement of the power of the state"—from Napoleon to Stalin and Hitler. In Nietzschean language, the text speaks of "the growing omnipotence of the state" and of "the strange and terrifying growth of the modern state" seeking to impose total domination on populations. In the case of German fascism, the book denounces the striving for "a technological world empire," for a "religion of anti-Christian (or spurious Christian) technology"—a striving which has not come to an end in 1945.[19] However, violent revolutionaries—today called "terrorists"—only replicate the striving for total control and the elimination of dissent. Camus carefully distinguishes genuine rebellion from violent revolution. A genuine rebellion, he notes, introduces a breach in the totalizing apparatus of power; it testifies to the unique dignity of human beings and also to something "common to all men which eludes the world of power." Ultimately, rebellion involves both a negation and an affirmation: it rejects the dominant nihilism and all forms of complicity in violent destruction and mayhem; at the same time, it upholds and cherishes life, fully aware of human limits: "The affirmation of a limit, a dignity, and a beauty common to all men entails the necessity of extending this value to embrace everything and everyone."[20]

These comments lead Camus to the most inspiring part of his book: his "Thought at the Meridian." As he observes, rebellion assigns a limit to oppression and totalizing power; in doing so, it acknowledges the dignity common to all human beings. It places in the center of its frame of reference "an obvious complicity among men, a common texture, the solidarity of chains, a communication between human being and human being which makes men similar and united" (in their differences). By contrast, murder or mayhem "cuts the world in two"; it sacrifices commonality by "consecrating difference in blood." What motivates the rebel is an ethical impulse, a desire for concrete interhuman justice. "If injustice is bad for the rebel," we read, "it is not because it contradicts an eternal idea of justice, but because it perpetuates the silent hostility that separates the oppressor from the oppressed. It kills the small part of existence that can be realized on this earth through the mutual understanding of men." All totalizing regimes proceed by way of monologue "preached from the top of lonely mountains"; but "on the stage as in reality, monologue precedes death." In rebellion, freedom and solidarity necessarily cohere. Thus, the rebel requires the freedom to act against injustice—which excludes "the right to destroy the existence and freedom of others." Camus sums up his argument in these lines: "It is then possible to say that rebellion, when it develops into destruction, is illogical. Claiming the unity of the human condition, it is a force of life, not of death. Its most profound logic is . . . the logic of creation."[21]

Dissent in Community

The preceding discussion has highlighted the difference between two main forms of dissent or critical resistance: on the one hand, libertarian social Darwinism, and on the other, ethically motivated conscientious resistance. In the former case, resistance aims to further the pursuit of particular, more or less self-centered interests; in the latter case, it serves to advance in some fashion the public interest or the "common good." The first type is enacted for the sake of a particular private benefit; the second involves an appeal from a corrupted or oppressive public life to a reformed and more legitimate public regime. Differently phrased: resistance is directed in one instance against community as such, while in the other instance it involves dissent within (or for the sake of) community. As I should add, what matters here is not whether resistance is the work of a solitary individual or a group of like-minded individuals. The issue concerns the purpose of action, not the number of agents.

My presentation, I trust, leaves no doubt about my own preferences in this matter: while I find social Darwinism and selfish libertarianism deeply flawed, my sympathy is with public-spirited resistance—as exemplified in the lifework of Thoreau, Gandhi, and Camus. To lend added support to this preference I want to mention—by way of conclusion—two other examples: one taken from the dawn of Western civilization and the other from its dusk (or the time of its derailment). The first example involves Socrates and his conflict with the collective opinion of his city, Athens. As is well known, Socrates was accused of impiety (of not honoring the gods of the city) and of corrupting young people by disturbing reigning beliefs. The story is reported both in the *Apology* and in the *Criton*, and both texts reveal the central issue: the clash between an upright critical mind and a lethargic or manipulated public opinion. In the *Apology*, Socrates drives home this issue by asking whether the multitude or public opinion are always right in questions of ethics or justice, as his accusers claim. But how could this be, seeing that the multitude never bothers to inquire into these questions—whereas he, Socrates, has made such inquiry his all-consuming business? Regarding the issue of impiety, he has always followed an inner spiritual guidance—as even his accusers acknowledge—and how could this practice entail a rejection of the divine? In the end, Socrates reluctantly acknowledges a near-insoluble conflict between the public and critical dissent. "The fact is that no man in the world will come off safe who honestly opposes either you or any other multitude, and tries to hinder the many unjust and illegal doings in a state."[22]

Recounting the final hours before Socrates's death, *Criton* is a paean to the dignity of the human spirit in confrontation with collective prejudice and meanness. As is clear from the preceding dialogue, the charges brought by his accusers against him were unjust, and so was the final verdict of death handed down by the court. The basic issue here becomes the relation between the city—or the opinion of the multitude in a city—and the rule of justice. Was it the case that, due to the injustice inflicted on him, the rule of justice and the bond linking Socrates and the city had been broken and he was now free to escape the verdict by seeking refuge elsewhere—as his friend Criton suggests? But, by seeking to escape the verdict, Socrates himself would commit an injustice and thus descend to the level of the ignorant and vindictive multitude. This Socrates refuses to do, arguing: "We must not do wrong in return, or do evil to anyone in the world, however we may be treated by them." With this refusal, Socrates seals his fate—but he also maintains the idea and the bond of justice linking him to the city (which he had never left throughout his life). With his final action, Socrates strongly affirms his freedom—a freedom from injustice though not from the city and its ethical bond of solidarity. In dissenting from the multitude, his aim was not to destroy the city but to lift it up to the rule of justice without which a city cannot endure.[23]

The second example is taken from the time of modern civilization's derailment, when the modern state in Germany decayed into Nazi totalitarianism. Although there were pockets of dissent acting sporadically since the beginning of the regime, more organized forms of resistance surfaced before and during the course of World War II, and mainly within the military establishment. Even prior to the outbreak of the war, a group of officers sought to avert the looming disaster through political means; but the fast pace of events nullified their effort. Once the war was underway, there were repeated acts of resistance—in the form of assassination plots or suicide bombing attempts—planned or carried out by members of the higher officer

corps; but unforeseen circumstances always foiled these moves. In evaluating
these attempts, one has to take into account the extreme complexity of the
situation: the fact that military officers are bound by an oath of loyalty to
their country—an oath weighing especially heavily during wartime (and even
more so when the war was turning against Germany). One can be certain
that many or most officers involved in the resistance felt deeply this burden
of loyalty, while also being profoundly troubled by the growing barbarism
and criminality of the country's leaders. Thus, like Antigone long ago, they
were starkly conflicted between two loyalties: one to their "city" or political regime, and the other to the higher "rule of justice" and the "better
angels" of their country. This may account for some of their prevarications
and periods of indecision. The resistance movement against Hitler came to
a head in 1943 with Operation Valkyrie. One of the members of the plot
was a young staff officer, Graf von Stauffenberg (who in addition to his
scruples as an officer was also troubled by religious scruples). The plot was
enacted on July 20 but failed in its main goal; Stauffenberg and most of
his fellow resisters were executed.[24]

As one should add, anti-Nazi resistance was not exclusively in the
hands of military officers but also had civilian support in some quarters.
One instance was the antiwar campaign "White Rose" launched and carried forward by some students and teachers at the University of Munich in
early 1943 (a campaign that was quickly crushed and its leaders executed).
Another important civilian figure in the resistance movement was Dietrich
Bonhoeffer (1906–1945), a Lutheran pastor, theologian, and lifelong anti-
fascist. Bonhoeffer had studied theology in Berlin where he discovered the
neo-orthodox "dialectical theology" of Karl Barth. Subsequently he spent
a year at Union Theological Seminary in New York under the guidance of
Reinhold Niebuhr. After returning to Germany, he immediately launched
an attack against Hitler, publicly calling the *Führer* a *Verführer* (seducer or
pied piper). In early 1934, at a gathering of Lutheran clergy, he endorsed
the so-called "Barmen declaration" (drafted by Barth), which insisted that
Christ and not a political despot was the head of the church. At the same
time, he was instrumental in founding the "Confessing Church," standing
in opposition to Protestant clergy co-opted by the Nazi regime.[25]

The regime was quick to retaliate and to harass Bonhoeffer in his
clerical and academic activities. In 1936 his teaching position in Berlin
was revoked, forcing him into the role of an itinerant clergyman. At the
beginning of the war, he became acquainted with members of a resistance
movement located in the heart of German military intelligence (so-called

Abwehr), a linkage which made him familiar with assassination plots. As in the case of Stauffenberg, Bonhoeffer's scruples were deeply nurtured by his faith and the divine commandment against killing. As he wrote in his *Ethics*: "When a man takes guilt upon himself in responsibility, he imputes his guilt to himself and no one else. Before himself he is acquitted by his conscience, but before God he hopes only for grace."[26] Arrested in April 1943 he spent a year and a half in military prison. In February 1945 he was moved to Buchenwald where he was executed by hanging on April 9 (just two weeks before the camp was liberated).

Many decades have passed since the great war and in the meantime, one says, totalitarianism has disappeared. But has it really? Or has it returned in different guises? Probably one should not underestimate the ingenuity and resourcefulness of the modern state—of that "cold monster" and "horse of death" bemoaned by Nietzsche. Quite likely, the great Leviathan has not been caught or tamed; even when outwardly assuming innocuous airs, it may still seethe inside with fires of destruction. Moreover, since the totalitarianism of the last century, the Leviathan has acquired new and unheard-of methods: unprecedented technological powers of mayhem, unlimited capabilities of surveillance, and uncanny forms of brainwashing and "double-speak." Camus's *The Rebel* contains some dark lines which one needs to ponder: "The sources of life and creation seem exhausted. Fear paralyzes a Europe peopled with phantoms and machines."[27] What is the meaning of the politics of fear recently gripping the West? What should one make of the cult of violence and death evident in movies, video games, and often in real life? What does the cult presage? Here, by way of conclusion, a line from Nietzsche's "The Wanderer and His Shadow": "Rather perish than hate and fear. And twice rather perish than make oneself hated and feared—this must someday become the highest maxim for every single commonwealth too."[28]

6

NEO-LIBERALISM AND ITS CRITICS

Voices from East and West

> The clear consciousness of a communal life, in all its implications, constitutes the idea of democracy.
>
> —John Dewey

Heraclitus notwithstanding, history is not just random flux. Apart from its great or memorable events, every historical period also pays tribute to certain guideposts or guiding ideas—what skeptics call its *idola fori* or idols of the marketplace. Looking at our contemporary age, it is not difficult to pinpoint a guiding, and probably *the* guiding, idea endorsed almost universally by people around the world: that of "liberal democracy." Although originating in Western societies, the idea today is circulating as an orienting loadstar among people in Africa, the Middle East, as well as South and East Asia. As can readily be seen, the guidepost is actually a composite phrase combining the two terms "liberal" and "democracy." Yet, despite possible contrasts, the two terms in recent times have been basically conflated or amalgamated—with the result that, in the view of both ordinary people and leading intellectuals, the "democratic" component has become redundant or been absorbed without a rest in the dominant "liberal" idea. This conflation is particularly evident in, and traceable to, modern economics (with its own idols of the "market"). In large measure, the ongoing process of globalization is fueled by the idea of "neo-liberalism"—a version of the liberal tradition which insists on "downsizing" political (including democratic) oversight for the sake of promoting individual or corporate "free enterprise."

This preponderance of liberal or neo-liberal agendas is by no means fortuitous. Taking a broad view, the entire trajectory of modern Western history can be seen as a movement of progressive human "liberation," above all liberation from clerical and autocratic modes of control. This trajectory was present already in the work of Thomas Hobbes, in his rupture with classical and medieval conceptions of community. The movement was carried forward by John Locke with his accent on the persistence of "natural rights"—especially the right to equal liberty—in the confines of an established commonwealth. The latter emphasis was deepened and fleshed out by later liberal thinkers, like John Stuart Mill and Benjamin Constant—whose arguments in favor of minimal government (laissez-faire) were by then powerfully buttressed by the rise of capitalism and modern market economics.

Small wonder that, in view of this long-standing trajectory, individual freedom became at last a catchword or shibboleth. As we know, the Western world calls itself, somewhat boastfully, the "Free World," while America celebrates itself as the "land of the free." As a corollary of this development, democracy as a political regime has come to be equated with an arena of free individual choice—that is, with liberal or libertarian democracy. But how plausible is this outcome? Has freedom in the modern world completely replaced such traditional categories as virtue and the "good life"—with the result that Aristotle's distinction between just and unjust regimes would be leveled into that between free and unfree forms of life? In the following I want to pursue this line of thought. In a first step, I shall outline the meaning of liberal or "neo-liberal" democracy, as it is defined by some contemporary theorists or philosophers. Subsequently I want to examine efforts to correct this neo-liberal conception, turning first to the South Asian and next to the East Asian context. By way of conclusion I shall review again the relation between liberalism and democracy.

Minimal or Neo-Liberal Democracy

As previously indicated, liberalism has a long history in the course of which it has assumed many different shapes and shadings. During the early period, the time of Hobbes and Locke, liberalism—in the sense of the defense of "natural" individual rights—served precariously as an adjunct or supplement to monarchical and even absolutist regimes. In the post-revolutionary era (roughly after 1800), liberalism became affiliated with various republican or democratic regimes—but in such a manner that the latter would progressively be trumped by the former (a development in which, as stated, the rise of capitalism played a major role). In the opinion of nineteenth-century liberals, the role of government—including democratic government—was meant to be minimal: seen chiefly as protectors of private property, political regimes were said to "govern best when governing least." The dismal experiences of the twentieth century with populist and totalitarian governments have reinforced this liberal preference for political or public minimalism—despite occasional concessions to "welfare" programs during times of economic hardship. As a result of these experiences and developments, the notion of individual freedom has come to be equated preponderantly with "negative liberty" (to use Isaiah Berlin's phrase) or the freedom to be left alone—with only limited allowance made for active or "positive freedom" (mainly on the level of voting rights and lobbying). In his study of John Dewey (who opposed this entire trend), Raymond Boisvert has sketched the stereotype of the minimalist liberal: "an individual with no roots and little connectedness to community; . . . a highly competitive individual fixated on narrow purposes whose practice is marked by expedience rather than conventional ethics."[1]

On a sophisticated level, aspects of democratic minimalism can be found even in the writings of theorists or intellectuals otherwise strongly committed to democratic politics. An example is Robert Dahl's celebrated text *A Preface to Democratic Theory* (first published in 1956). In the very introduction to his study, Dahl delineates two basic approaches in this field: a "maximizing" theory (relying either on ethical principles or formal axioms) and a purely "descriptive-empirical" and to that extent minimalizing approach. Traditional political theory, he notes, has tended to be "maximizing" by emphasizing "internal checks"—such as conscience and ethical dispositions—to restrain possible excesses of governmental power. Prerevolutionary writers in particular, he says, insisted upon "moral virtue among citizens as a necessary condition for republican government," a condition which needed to be cultivated through "hortatory religion, sound education, and honest government." This approach, however, has gone out of fashion since the revolutionary period and, in America, since the writings of James Madison. In Dahl's presentation, Madison proceeded to sideline the earlier "maximizing" approach which must have been still "a common assumption of his time." From Madison's perspective, the traditional ethical approach was simply no longer viable given the increasingly competitive and interest-based character of modern politics. Moreover, even if occasionally operative, ethical constraints were no longer reliable given the strength of individual ambitions. Hence, for both Madison and Dahl, modern governments require not traditional but "external [or procedural] checks" to restrain oppressive tendencies. As can readily be seen, however, procedural checks are themselves the result of contractual arrangements and hence dependent on changing individual preferences.[2]

Another example of a democratic theorist leaning in the minimalist direction is Giovanni Sartori, well known for his text *The Theory of Democracy Revisited* (which is a sequel to his earlier *Democratic Theory*, of 1962). Like Dahl's study, Sartori's text distinguishes at the outset between a "prescriptive" or normative conception and a "descriptive" or empirical conception—with the latter version involving greatly reduced demands on democratic politics. In his view, to introduce normative expectations is likely to overburden the democratic regime such as to render it unviable: "To bring morality into politics is akin to playing with fire—as we have only too well rediscovered since Hegel theorized a 'political ethos' or *Sittlichkeit*." In view of the alleged danger associated with public ethics, Sartori prefers to employ "minimalist" language and to leave phrases like "political morality, social morality, professional ethics" aside. What he finds particularly unhelpful or obnoxious is any association of democracy with public affection or Aristotelian-type friendship—something he derisively calls "demophily." As he insists: "Since real-world democracy consists (this is what renders it real) of a democratic machinery, democracy can do well without demophily." Democratic machinery coincides for him—and many other empirical theorists—with voting behavior, pursuit of individual interests through pressure groups and political parties, and public policy-making on the basic of these interests. Comprising this battery of elements, the democratic machinery basically yields what he calls "demo-power," that is, the power of the people, or predominant segments of the people, to implement and make effective prevailing interests: "Democracy begins with demo-power."[3]

An even more resolutely minimalist approach is propagated by a perspective which, in recent times, has increasingly gained prominence in the social sciences: "rational choice theory." This outlook basically transfers neo-classical economic assumptions to social and political life; under the aegis of "neo-liberalism," the perspective is fast emerging as something like a dominant global ideology. As can readily be seen, what is jeopardized or called into question by this model is not only public ethics but politics, particularly democratic politics, as such. For, even when seen as a minimally shared regime, democracy is bound to be a burden or hindrance for the ambitions of an unrestrained economic agenda. No one has articulated this burden more forcefully than William Riker, a founder of this model, in his book *Liberalism against Populism* (of 1982). In this text, the term "populism" stands for an interventionist or perhaps "Jacobin" type of democracy—in a manner which immediately renders democracy suspect (if compared with liberalism). As Riker states at the outset: "The theory of social [or rational] choice is a theory about the way the tastes, preferences, or values of individual persons are amalgamated and summarized into the choice of a collective group or society." Since these preferences are not ethically ranked, the primary focus is on something measurable or quantifiable: in economics monetary profit, in politics "the theory of voting," which is the core of liberal (or libertarian) democracy, barring any interference with voting preferences. Like Dahl, Riker distinguishes between a normative-ethical and an empirical or "analytical" conception of politics—placing rational choice clearly in the second category: the model is "an analytical theory about the way the natural world can [and does] work and what kind of outputs that world can yield."[4]

Again like Dahl, though with modified accents, Riker delineates two different genealogies of modern democracy: a "liberal or Madisonian" type and a "populist or Rousseauist" type. In the liberal (or libertarian) version, he notes, "The function of voting is to control officials, and *nothing else*"—meaning by "nothing else" the absence of positive political programs promoting something like the common good. As he adds, this Madisonian definition "is *logically* complete, and there is nothing to add. Madison said nothing about the quality of popular decision, whether good or bad." By contrast, "populists"—presumably following Rousseau—desire a more active, participatory role of the people and a politics that creates "a moral and collective body" endowed with "life and will," especially the (in)famous "general will." At this point, Riker endorses wholeheartedly Isaiah Berlin's notion of "negative liberty" and his indictment that "positive liberty, which appears initially innocuous, is the root of tyranny" or oppression. Tellingly, Riker also alludes to some ideological background—not unaffected by the geopolitics of the Cold War. "No government," he asserts, "that has eliminated economic freedom has been able to attain or keep democracy." On the other hand, "economic liberty is also an end in itself because capitalism is the driving force for the increased efficiency and technological innovation that has produced in two centuries both a vast increase in the wealth of capitalist nations and a doubling of the average life span of their citizens." Although acknowledging that it may be viewed as "minimalist" by some, Riker concludes that liberal or Madisonian democracy is "the only kind of democracy actually attainable" or feasible in our world.[5]

Beyond Minimalism: Voices from South Asia

In large measure, liberal democracy—in the sense of a minimalist, libertarian regime (or non-regime)—tends to occupy center stage in recent Western social and political thought. As it is important to note, this has not always been the case. During important phases of Western political development, minimalist liberal democracy has been criticized or contested by able thinkers and public intellectuals. One such phase was the American colonial period when the Puritan John Winthrop proposed the formation of an ethical-communitarian republic in Massachusetts Bay. Another, post-revolutionary, phase was the era of "Jacksonian democracy" when the ideal of an egalitarian republic was pitted against the laissez-faire ambitions of the emerging manufacturing elite (epitomized by the Bank of America). On a theoretical or philosophical plane, however, the most important development was the rise of "pragmatism" in the late nineteenth century, and especially John Dewey's eloquent defense of "radical" democracy as an antidote to laissez-faire liberalism. In Boisvert's words: for Dewey "democracy as an ideal for community life is not a mere provision for a minimal state which simply leaves citizens alone. Such an individualistic ideal is inimical to the kind of *associated* living which is democratic." To quote Dewey himself: "The clear consciousness of a communal life, in all its implications, constitutes the idea of democracy."[6]

For present purposes, given the contemporary global expansion of liberal (or neo-liberal) democracy, I want to turn my attention to non-Western intellectual contexts. An important context of this kind is South Asia and particularly India, the home of Mahatma Gandhi. As is well known, Gandhi was not only an astute politician or public leader but also a thinker or intellectual with deep insight into public affairs, including the requisites of democracy. On the latter issue he has pronounced himself repeatedly, but perhaps most forcefully and pithily in his early book of 1909 titled *Hind Swaraj* (or *Indian Home Rule*). In this text, Gandhi takes to task forms of democracy found in Western countries which are often upheld as shining models to the rest of the world. Concentrating his attention particularly on the British model, he delineates a long list of shortcomings or defects, ranging from the venality of parliament, or its subservience to vested interests, to the fluctuating whims of public opinion under the impact of power-hungry politicians or businessmen. Surveying these and a host of related blemishes, Gandhi does not hesitate to trace the malaise to a central underlying cause: the unrestrained pursuit of self-interest and self-indulgence, at the cost of shared ethical commitments to the public good. To be sure, as he acknowledges, modern life—even life in corrupt democracies—has brought greater freedom for many people in different strata of society; this advance, however, is marred and nearly eclipsed by prevailing abuses. In terms of *Hind Swaraj*, the main problem is the sway of self-centered materialism, the fact that people in the modern West "make bodily welfare the [sole] object of life." As the text starkly depicts the situation:

> This civilization takes note neither of morality [*niti*] nor of religion [*dharma*]. . . . [It] seeks to increase bodily comforts, and it fails miserably even in doing so. This civilization is irreligion [*adharma*], and it has taken such a hold on the people in Europe that those who are in it appear to be half mad. . . . They keep up their energy by intoxication.[7]

The remedy proposed in *Hind Swaraj* for this state of affairs is precisely self-rule or *swaraj*—which does not mean selfish rule or promotion of self-centered ambitions but rather the ability to rein in such ambitions for the benefit of the common good, that is, the good of all people. As Gandhi points out, egocentrism or individual self-seeking is contrary not only to ethical and spiritual "rightness" (one sense of *dharma*) but also to the teachings of practically all the great religions of the world—including (next to Hinduism) Christianity, Islam, Judaism, and Zoroastrianism (he might have added Buddhism). What all these religions try to teach us, he writes, is "that we should remain passive [or reticent] about worldly pursuits and active about godly [or ethical] pursuits, that we should set a limit to our worldly ambition, and that our religious [or dharmic] ambitions should be illimitable." Despite differences of accent or detail, all religions and ethical-spiritual paths can thus be seen as "different roads converging to the same point." People following these paths are liable to achieve not "civilization in name only" but genuine culture or civilization befitting free and responsible human beings. In Gandhi's terse formulation: "Civilization is that mode of conduct which points out to human beings the path of duty. Performance of ethical duty . . . means to attain mastery over our mind and our passions. In so doing, we come to know ourselves." Even more importantly: in so doing, we come to rule ourselves both as individuals and as people. The clear implication of this view is a new understanding of democracy: in the sense not of the pursuit of individual or collective self-interest but of a transformative popular self-rule (that is, rule of people over themselves) or *swaraj*: "It is *swaraj* when we learn to rule ourselves."[8]

Although composed relatively early in his life (and during an arduous sea voyage from London to South Africa), the basic tenets of *Hind Swaraj* remained firm guideposts during Gandhi's mature years. Although willing to revise minor details, he never disavowed his early text; in fact, he reconfirmed its central argument on repeated occasions in subsequent years. A few examples should suffice to document this continuity. In his "Constructive Program" submitted to the Indian National Congress in 1941, Gandhi strongly reaffirmed his commitment to *swaraj*, explaining the meaning of the term as denoting "complete independence through truth [*satya*] and non-violence [*ahimsa*]" and "without distinction of race, color or creed." A letter written to Jawaharlal Nehru a few years later made explicit reference to the text of 1909, stating: "I have said that I still stand by the system of government envisaged in *Hind Swaraj*." In retrospect, what appeared to Gandhi as the central lesson of his book was the emphasis on ethical self-rule and self-restraint, on a conception of individual and public agency performed within the limits of rightness or truth (*satya*) and nonviolent generosity toward others. The most dramatic and direct application of the idea of *swaraj* came in his "Quit India" speech delivered in Bombay in 1942. In that speech, Gandhi—now the leader of a nationwide *satyagraha* (civil resistance relying on "truth power")—contrasted his vision of Indian self-rule with the kind of freedom and political rulership found in Britain and the Western world, saying:

> I do not regard England, or for that matter America, as free countries. They are free after their own fashion: free to hold in bondage the colored races of the earth. . . . According to my own interpretation of that freedom, I am constrained to say: they are strangers to that freedom which their [own] poets and teachers have described.[9]

Profiled against dominant Western approaches, Gandhi's idea of *swaraj* discloses a conception of democracy—an ethical conception—sharply at variance with interest-based models of liberal or libertarian democracy. Despite his fondness for Western writers like Ruskin, Thoreau, and Tolstoy, Gandhi was not a radical individualist (in the modern liberal or neo-liberal sense) ready to separate a vast arena of private freedom from a narrowly circumscribed, perhaps minimalist, public-democratic domain. Faithful to older philosophical traditions (both in India and the West), he preferred to stress a qualitative distinction between modes of human and political conduct—a distinction that cannot readily be collapsed into modern private/public or internal/external polarities. Without blandly fusing individual and society or subordinating one to the other, his thought was able to hold the two elements in fruitful, perhaps tensional balance. This aspect is clearly shown in another letter Gandhi wrote to Nehru in 1945. Picking up Nehru's suggestion regarding the importance of human and social development, he fully agreed that it was crucial to "bring about man's highest intellectual, economic, political and moral development," that is, the "flourishing" of all human abilities. The basic issue was how to accomplish this goal. For Gandhi this was impossible without thorough attention to rightness (*dharma*) and without civil engagement and responsibility. Echoing Aristotle, and countering the modern Western focus on self-centered individualism carried over from an atomistic "state of nature" into society, he wrote: "Man is not born to live in isolation but is essentially a social animal independent *and* interdependent. No one can or should ride on another's back." A similar view was expressed in an interview of summer 1946 where Gandhi stated that, although the individual does count in important ways, this "does not exclude dependence and willing help from neighbors or from the world. It will be a free and voluntary play of mutual forces."[10]

In speaking of interconnectedness and the "play of mutual forces" Gandhi displays an affinity with the spirit of Jamesian and Deweyan pragmatism. But the parallel can be carried further. Like William James and Dewey, and perhaps even more emphatically, Gandhi was an ethical and spiritual pragmatist, in the great tradition of Indian spirituality. As is well known, the most important source of inspiration for Gandhi throughout his life was the Bhagavad Gita, a text which delineates several paths (or *yoga*s) guiding toward liberation and blessedness (in the sense of flourishing). Among these paths, Gandhi deliberately chose the path of action or praxis (*karma yoga*) demanding continuous ethical engagement in the affairs of the world. Again like Dewey, he did not assume that human beings are free and equal by nature (or in an original "state of nature"); rather, freedom and equality for him were achievements requiring steady practice—a practice involving change of not only outward conditions but primarily self-transformation. In Gandhi's own words, freedom is not an instant boon but is "attained only by constant heart-churn" or self-giving in service to others. In the words of Ramashray Roy, in his thoughtful book *Self and Society*, *karma yoga* for Gandhi was not just a form of activism or worldly busyness but rather a soteriological path or a process of sanctification which sees performance of action as sacred duty: "This sacred duty lies in exerting oneself to the benefit of others, that is, service."[11] Viewed from this angle, achievement of self-rule or *swaraj* involves self-transcendence and a diligent training in the ways of freedom. In a manner akin to Deweyan political thought, pursuit of liberating paths (or *yogas*) demands steady practice and habituation, facilitated by sound education. In a more directly Aristotelian view, such practice revolves around the nurturing of a set of virtues—which Gandhi reformulated under the rubric of ethical and spiritual "vows" (*yamas*).

Comparing Gandhian *swaraj* with dominant forms of modern Western thought, the differences are stark and obvious. What needs to be noted right away is the distance of *swaraj* from prevalent modern conceptions of freedom: those of "negative" and "positive" liberty. As can readily be seen, neither of these options shows kinship with Gandhian *swaraj*. Even when highly spiritualized, negative liberty still bears traces of individual self-centeredness, while the positive type—in stressing worldly activism—seems ignorant of self-restraint, releasement, and nonattachment to the fruits of action. This distance has been clearly pinpointed by Ramashray Roy. As he observers, negative liberty insists on social aloofness, on the retreat into a private realm often coinciding with selfishness or the wanton "satisfaction of desires." On the other hand, while emphasizing social and political engagement, positive liberty sidesteps the task of self-curtailment and self-transcendence by extolling the benefits of collectively chosen goals. For Roy, it was "Gandhi's genius" to have squarely faced this dilemma and have shown an exit from this binary dilemma. The central point of Gandhian *swaraj*, he notes, was the emphasis on self-rule as a transformation process—whereby people are able to rule not so much over others as over themselves.[12]

The arguments regarding freedom or liberty can readily be transferred to the basic meaning of democracy. The difference between Gandhian *swaraj* and the liberal-minimalist conception of democracy has been ably highlighted by the Gandhi scholar Ronald Terchek, especially in his essay titled "Gandhi and Democratic Theory." Right at the outset Terchek states the crux of the matter: that democracy for Gandhi was not merely "procedural" or minimal but "substantive" in the sense of being grounded in a nonoppressive way of life. He cites Gandhi himself to the effect that, under democracy, "the weakest should have the same opportunity as the strongest. And this can never happen except through [political, social, and psychological] non-violence."[13] Basically, for the Mahatma, democracy is a regime not organized or imposed "from the top down" (or from the state down) but one nurtured "from the bottom up." This explains his emphasis on village life and village self-government (through councils or panchayats), as well as on economic decentralization and local industries. In Terchek's presentation, Gandhi believed that the means of production (at least of the basic necessaries of life) should remain ultimately in the hands of the people—and not be relinquished or alienated to corporate elites. In contrast to the rampant competition unleashed by the capitalist market, he stressed the need to cultivate cooperative dispositions so that the brute "struggle for survival" would be transmuted into a "struggle for mutual service" or "mutual existence."[14]

Beyond Minimalism: Voices from East Asia

When turning from India to East Asia, similar reservations regarding minimal democracy can readily be found. The critique of radical individualism proceeds there mainly (though not exclusively) on Confucian premises, a philosophy well known for its emphasis on human relationships. Given the essential relatedness of human beings, freedom for Confucians cannot mean either internal retreat or external manipulation and domination. This point is eloquently made by the Chinese American scholar Tu Weiming. As he observes, Confucianism basically opposes the binary scheme of negative and positive liberty, that is, the construal of freedom in terms of either private self-withdrawal or domineering self-enhancement. "It rejects," he writes, "both an introspective affirmation of the self as an isolable and complacent ego *and* an unrestrained attachment to the external world for the sake of a limitless expansion of one's manipulative power." In lieu of these alternatives, the Confucian "way" or *tao*—akin to Gandhian *swaraj*—involves an "unceasing process of self-transformation as a communal act," and thus a linkage of ethics and social engagement whose seasoning effect "can ultimately free us from the constrictions of the privatized ego." As can readily be seen, human freedom from this angle is limited or circumscribed not by the state or external procedures but by the ability for ethical transformation, that is, the ability of people to rule themselves rather than ruling others.[15]

In addition to social engagement and connectedness, Confucianism also fosters the relatedness between human beings and nature as well as the "mutuality between man and Heaven." Ultimately, Tu Weiming notes, the Confucian trajectory points to the human reconciliation with "Heaven, Earth, and the myriad things"—with clearly spiritual or religious connotations. In an instructive manner, he also points to the Confucian stress on exemplification, that is, the need not merely to hold fine theories but to exemplify them in daily conduct. Despite his deep modesty, Confucius himself can be seen, and was seen, as an "exemplar" or "exemplary person" (*chün-tzu*) who taught the "way" not through abstract doctrines but through the testimony of responsible daily living. At this point, the affinity with Deweyan philosophy comes clearly into view—a fact which is perhaps not surprising given Dewey's extended visit to China after World War I.[16] As in the case of Gandhian *swaraj*, leading a responsible life in society involves self-restraint and the abandonment of domineering impulses. In Confucius's own words, humaneness or to be properly human (*jen*) means "to conquer oneself (*k'e-chi*) and to return to propriety (*fu-li*)." As Tu Weiming comments, however, the notion of "conquering oneself" should not be misconstrued in the sense of self-erasure in favor of heteronomous forces. The Confucian idea, he writes, does not mean "that one should engage in a bitter struggle" of conquest; rather, the concept of *k'e-chi* is "closely linked to the concept of self-cultivation (*hsiu-shen*)" or self-transformation and hence to the task of responsible and responsive social agency.[17]

More difficult to assess is the relation of Confucian thought to modern democracy seen as popular self-rule and self-government. In large measure, the difficulty arises from the fact that, in contrast to the Gandhian legacy, traditional Confucianism is silent on democracy and the political implications of human agency. This silence is often taken as evidence of the utter incompatibility of Confucian teachings and democratic regimes. In the words of the China scholar Ni Peinim: "The dominant view today still holds that Confucianism and democracy are like water and fire, totally incompatible and antagonistic to each other." According to this view, the former is "authoritarian, repressive, and typically associated with totalitarian policies, uniformity of ideology, social hierarchy, and discrimination against women"—while democracy is "the very opposite."[18] In a similar vein, Wm. Theodore de Bary has pointed out that, during much of the twentieth century, Confucianism "was made to stand for all that was backward and benighted in China: it bore all the burden of the past, charged with innumerable sins of the old order." When in 1989—he adds—the "Goddess of Democracy" was publicly displayed in Tiananmen Square, the display was a revolt not only against Communist repression but also against the older Confucian tradition.[19] In this context, traditional Confucian sayings like "The common people are the root or foundation of society" (from the *Shujing*) are widely regarded as pious placebos devoid of concrete political connotations.

At this point, it becomes important to ask what precisely is at issue. Does the claimed incompatibility prevail between Confucianism and democracy tout court, or between the former and a certain kind of liberalism or liberal democracy? In the latter case, the meaning of "liberal" and "liberalism" becomes decisive. Do these terms refer to the ethical kind of liberalism which can be traced from Montesquieu and Hegel all the way to Dewey's definition of democracy as an ethical community? Or do we mean the self-seeking, laissez-faire libertarianism which ultimately reduces social life to an atomistic state of nature? In the former case—making room for creative adjustments—it seems quite possible to envisage a harmony between Confucianism and modern democracy. In the latter case, harmony or compatibility is clearly excluded—but only because self-centered liberalism is at variance with democracy as such (or only allows for minimalist democracy). The need for a creative adjustment or rethinking of traditional teachings is today acknowledged by many Confucian scholars, especially by such "New Confucians" as Tu Weiming and Liu Shu-hsien. As the latter has aptly stated: "We have to reject the tradition in order to reaffirm the ideal of the tradition."[20] However, such a rethinking of Confucian teachings also requires, as a complementary move, a rethinking of prevalent modern Western ideas—away from the egocentric preferences of democratic minimalism in the direction of a responsible democratic ethos. As it appears to me, such a double rethinking is admirably manifest in the writings of the China scholar Henry Rosemont Jr.

In several of his texts, Rosemont has eloquently castigated the notion of an egocentric individualism patterned on capitalist economics. As he writes at one point (in a passage with patent Deweyan echoes): "For most of the world's peoples, there are no disembodied minds, nor autonomous individuals; human relationships govern and structure most of our lives, to the point that unless there are at least two human beings, there can be no human beings." As one should note, however, this critique of egocentrism does not induce Rosemont to reject democracy as such. As he states in one of his more well-known writings, *A Chinese Mirror*, what he is proposing or suggesting is not a return to autocracy but rather "a somewhat different philosophical view of democracy"—a view more in line with an ethical conception of both liberalism and democracy.[21] The concrete contours of this alternative view are spelled out by Rosemont in another text which intriguingly joins Confucian "relationism" with the pragmatic account of a shared way of life. From this alternative perspective, he states, democracy—including an ethically liberal democracy—might be described as a regime in which every member has the right and duty "to participate in public affairs" and "to take the public welfare of all the other members of society as one's own." As one can see, democracy here is elevated to the height of the vision of a Montesquieu, Tocqueville, and Dewey. To conclude with another passage from *A Chinese Mirror*, even more distinctly Deweyan in orientation: In a properly constituted democratic community, "the desired would not be equated with the desirable, and democratic participation—being a citizen—would involve engaging in collective dialogue about the appropriate means for achieving agreed-upon ends."[22]

Concluding Remarks

In the preceding pages, I have delineated critiques of minimalist liberal democracy, focusing on Gandhian and Confucian teachings. These critical voices could readily be expanded or multiplied. One of the noteworthy developments in Asia in recent decades has been the upsurge of a "new" kind of Buddhism, an outlook which shifts the earlier accent on monastic retreat in the direction of a more worldly engagement and participation. Here again, the twin pitfalls of negative and positive liberty are bypassed (at least in intent). While transgressing the bounds of a purely internal liberation, the turn to engagement carefully steers clear of public manipulation or the pursuit of social blueprints, thus maintaining the central Buddhist focus on "self-emptying" (*sunyata*) and self-transcendence (toward others).[23] Under very different auspices and in a different idiom, tendencies pointing in a similar direction can also be found in strands of contemporary Islamic thought. In this context, the traditional biblical injunction to "pursue justice" above everything else still serves as a powerful incentive to foster an ethically vibrant public life. However, contrary to "fundamentalist" misconstruals, this incentive does not automatically translate into theocracy or clerical despotism. On the contrary, precisely because justice needs to be done in concrete times and places, ordinary people are called upon to act as "vice-regents" or (more prosaically) as co-participants in the formation of ethically just modes of politics. In recent times, the idea of a basic compatibility of

Islam and democracy has been defended by a number of able intellectuals, from Muhammad Iqbal to Abdulaziz Sachedina and Abdolkarim Soroush. In Iqbal's pithy phrase: "Islam demands loyalty to God, not to thrones." Paraphrasing and amplifying this idea, the philosopher Soroush has stated: "No blessing is more precious for mankind than the free choice of the way of the prophets. But in the absence of this state of grace, nothing is better for humankind than [democratic] freedom. Because all free societies, whether religious or nonreligious, are properly humane."[24]

As indicated before, the critique of public minimalism is not restricted to non-Western contexts. On the contrary, some of the most eloquent critical voices have been precisely Western and, in fact, American. Just a few years ago, the American political theorist Michael Sandel issued a plea for a renewed "public philosophy" which would reconnect ethics and politics. What stands in the way of such a renewal, in his account, is the predominance of (what he calls) the "voluntarist conception of freedom," that is, the laissez-faire ideology of untrammeled self-seeking, which dispenses with the "difficult task" of cultivating civic dispositions. As an antidote to this ideology, Sandel pleads in favor of a "formative politics" concerned with the formation of ethical civic attitudes and practices; for (he says) "to share in self-rule requires that citizens possess, or come to acquire, certain civic virtues."[25]

In issuing this plea, of course, Sandel stands on the shoulders of a series of earlier American thinkers, including the journalist and public intellectual Walter Lippmann. Some seventy years ago, Lippmann had denounced the spreading cult of egocentric will power in economics and politics. As he noted in *The Good Society*, Western modernity had derailed when it moved to equate freedom with individual self-seeking. In opposition to this equation—the "doctrine of *laissez-faire*, let her rip, and the devil take the hindmost"—Lippmann invoked an older tradition of ethical liberalism congruent with public obligations. Borrowing a leaf from Aristotle as well as American pragmatism, his text observed: "There must be [in democracy] an habitual, confirmed, and well-nigh intuitive dislike of arbitrariness. There must be a strong desire to be just. [And] there must be a growing capacity to be just."[26]

However, the strongest American voice against the derailment into laissez-faire minimalism was John Dewey. As I have stated repeatedly, Dewey was relentless in critiquing a reckless individualism and in upholding social "relationism" and the need for civic bonds. As one should note well, his animus was directed not against liberalism as such, but against a minimalist version incompatible with democratic self-rule. Likewise, his target was not individual liberty (or individual selfhood) per se, but only its imprisonment in the Cartesian fortress of the "ego cogito." In the words of Raymond Boisvert: Whereas radical individualism connotes "both isolation and self-interestedness," "individuality" in the revised Deweyan sense identifies "the distinctive manner in which someone participates in communal life"; it recognizes "the irreducibility of community and the multiple perspectives associated with it."[27] Such individuality and the multiple perspectives to which it gives rise are not opposed to but actually constitutive of democratic life. Above all, what needs to be remembered is that, for Dewey, democracy is not a finished state but an ongoing process of "democratizing" pointing toward rich untapped horizons. Democracy, he states at one point, is "an end that has not been adequately realized in any country at any time. It is radical because it requires great change in existing social institutions, economic, legal and cultural." To this might be added his observation that, under democratic auspices, "the supreme test of all political institutions and industrial arrangements shall be the contribution they make to the all-round growth [or better: flourishing] of every member of society."[28]

A crucial aspect of the contribution is the avoidance of violence and brute power politics. As Dewey once remarked, in a very Gandhian spirit: "To take as far as possible every conflict which arises . . . out of the atmosphere and medium of force, of violence as a means of settlement, into that of discussion and of intelligence is to treat those who disagree—even profoundly—with us as those from whom we may learn and, in so far, as friends."[29] This disposition toward nonviolence, however, does not come easy. For Dewey, as we know, such a disposition or civic habit is not a ready-made "natural" endowment but a human potentiality requiring continuous struggle and lifelong educational cultivation.

INDIVIDUALIZED LIFE

The Plight of Narcissism

World alienation, and not self-alienation as Marx thought, has been
the hallmark of the modern age.

—Hannah Arendt

In a stunning text written during the Second World War, Max Horkheimer
and Theodor Adorno spoke provocatively of the "dialectic of enlightenment." With this expression, the authors introduced a disturbing connota-
tion into the terms of the phrase. While, in the usage of both Hegel and
Marx, "dialectic" signified a steady though stepwise historical advancement,
Horkheimer and Adorno pointed to the underside or costs of this trajectory; without denying a certain progressive movement in history, their text
alerted readers to the counterpoint of regress often unleashed by the same
movement. Likewise, "enlightenment"—celebrated by the modern Age of
Reason—was prone to give rise to countervailing trends, especially the
rise of instrumental rationality and the abuse of rational knowledge in the
pursuit of domineering agendas. What was perhaps most troubling in the
authors' formulation was that the end point of history could not be posi-
tively described or pinpointed and thus had necessarily the character of a
wager which was always threatened by defeat.[1]

The sketched counterpoint is nowhere more clearly evident than in
the vaunted lynchpin of Western modernity: the rise of human autonomy

or self-centered individualism. While, for champions of this rise, "premodern" society was basically "communitarian" if not collectivist in character, it was the achievement of Western modernity to liberate human beings from "external" or "heteronomous" constraints and thus to make possible the flourishing of individual freedom and selfhood. Major theoretical formulas—like "from status to contract" or "from community (*Gemeinschaft*) to society (*Gesellschaft*)"—have thought to capture this change.[2] But an unexpected dialectic took its toll. While in the early phases of modernity, individual autonomy was still socially nurtured and embedded, subsequent developments put the premium increasingly on "negative" (or disengaged) liberty, thus pushing individuals steadily into private self-enclosure. In the view of Horkheimer and Adorno, once privatized or atomized, modern freedom came to "boomerang" against itself by subjecting individuals to new and powerful heteronomies, especially in the fields of economics and technology. In the language of psychoanalysis, radical self-enclosure is termed "narcissism." In 1979, Christopher Lasch sounded the alarm by claiming that, by that time, narcissism was no longer an individual ailment but a social pathology or a public "culture."[3] In the meantime, this assessment has gained near-universal acceptance.

In the following, I shall first examine a more recent portrayal of this pathology: Zygmunt Bauman's *The Individualized Society* (2001). Next, to illustrate the progressive globalization of the pathology, I discuss a leading Indian psychologist, Ashis Nandy, and especially his *Regimes of Narcissism, Regimes of Despair* (2013). By way of conclusion, I turn to the spreading narcissism under the impact of the pandemic and finally to the possible restoration of public agency and a viable "public space" as recommended by Hannah Arendt.

Individualized Society

Zygmunt Bauman is known primarily for his notion of "liquid modernity," the argument that modernity coincides basically with a process of liquefaction or the relentless dissolution of stable positions and relationships. As he writes in his book of that title: "The whole of modernity stands out from preceding epochs by its compulsive and obsessive modernizing—and modernizing means liquefaction, melting and smelting." Foremost among the features that are "melted and smelted" are social institutions and especially "public spaces" suitable for the exercise of civic agency. In language reminiscent of

Horkheimer and Adorno, his book speaks of the dialectic of emancipation or the "mixed blessings of [modern] freedom." For Bauman, this dialectic becomes evident when the liberation of the individual (as a social being) is turned into "negative freedom" or the one-sided liberation "from" society and civic obligations. At this point, "individualization"—which is endemic to modernity—comes to clash with citizenship. Here is a telling passage:

> If the individual is the citizen's worst enemy, and if individual-ization spells trouble for citizenship and citizen-based politics, it is because the concerns and preoccupations of individuals *qua* individuals fill the public space to the brim. . . .
>
> [Now] the "public" is colonized by the "private"; "public interest" is reduced to curiosity about private lives of public fig-ures, and the art of public life is narrowed to the public display of private affairs and public confessions of private sentiments (the more intimate the better).[4]

The process of individualization—its overt and hidden costs—was further explored by Bauman in his *The Individualized Society*. As for the Frankfurt theorists, the issue for him is not the value of human individuality per se, of a life anchored in individual conscience and responsibility. The problem resides in egocentrism, that is, in the predominance of narcissistic self-enclosure shutting out civic interaction and interdependence. Like Lasch, Bauman speaks here of a "culture" of disengagement and disassociation, a condition which has as a corollary a crisis or breakdown of the ordinary routines of social life: "We speak of a 'cultural crisis' if the routine comes to be defied and breached too often to be seen as reliable, let alone to be taken for granted." Closely linked with disassociation is the growing habit of radical self-assertion, often producing a bellicose Hobbesian state of nature. Individual dominance, Bauman writes, is achieved "by removing the rules constraining one's own freedom of choice, while at the same time imposing as many restrictive rules as possible on the conduct of all others." In this combative situation, not everyone is equally able to impose his or her will power on others; thus, radical self-centered freedom inevitably leads to new hierarchies of domination coupled with the unfreedom of victims: "Thanks to the new techniques of disengagement, non-commitment, evasion and escape now at the disposal of [new] elites, the rest may be held in check, disabled and so deprived of their constraining ability simply by the utter vulnerability and precariousness of their situation." Due to the arbitrary willfulness of the new elites, the victims of individualized society are cast into a condition of insecurity, randomness, and disposability. In the words of Pierre Bourdieu: "Précarité est aujourd'hui partout."[5]

As a sharp-eyed political sociologist, Bauman clearly perceives the costs of individualization for politics, and especially for democracy. In a context of atomistic self-seekers, little or no room is left for considerations of the common good or the ethically good life. Individuals in that context, Bauman writes, tend to be "lukewarm, skeptical and wary of the 'common good,' of the 'good society' or 'just society.' What is the sense of *common* interests unless they let each individual satisfy her or his own?" What takes the place of the common good in individualized society is the accent on "human rights," tendentially construed in an egocentric or narcissistic way: "The only two useful things that 'public power' can be expected to deliver is to observe 'human rights,' that is, to let everyone go her or his own way, and to enable everyone to do it in peace—by guarding the safety of a person's body and possessions." Bauman speaks in this context of the "corrosion and disintegration" of democratic citizenship, citing a passage in Joel Roman's *La démocratie des individus* to the effect that "vigilance is degraded to the surveillance of goods, while general interest is no more than a syndicate of egoisms, engaging collective emotions and fear of the neighbor." Changing or transforming this atomistic condition is a steep task—and Bauman is quite ambivalent about its possibility. The odds in any case are against transformation. "In the land of individual freedom of choice," he muses, "the option to escape individualization and to refuse to participate in the individualizing game is emphatically *not* on the agenda." If this is the case, then the odds are also against a genuine democracy: "The prospects of the individualized actors being 're-embedded' in the republican body of citizenship are slim."[6]

Yet, ambivalence here does not give way to cynicism or despair. *The Individualized Society* also contains a chapter titled "Am I My Brother's Keeper?"—the question addressed by Cain to God after his attack on Abel. Bauman takes this question very seriously; in fact, he treats it as a basic human and social question. He refers to the ethical philosopher Emmanuel Levinas in whose view Cain's angry question was the beginning of all immorality and for whom it was clear that "I am my brother's keeper because my brother's well-being *depends* on what I do or refrain from doing." And as long as I recognize that dependence and accept the moral responsibility that fellows, I am "a moral person."

The question here becomes the relation between ethical aspirations and social constraints. On one level, Bauman accepts the validity of aspirations.

As he writes, Levinas erected "the need of the other, and the responsibility for meeting that need, into the cornerstone of morality—and the acceptance of that responsibility into the birth-act of the moral person." On the other hand, as an empirical sociologist, Bauman also perceives the vulnerability of the argument, especially if it is translated into "welfare state" policies. As he states bluntly, the welfare state today has everywhere a "bad press." This fact is based on a simple economic realization: namely, that "even if the new rules of the market game promise a rise in the total wealth of the nation, they also, inevitably, make inescapable the widening gap between those in the game and the rest who are left out." This gap shapes and even "overdetermines" the fortunes of the welfare state: "The rich and powerful see it as a bad investment and money wasted, while the less rich and powerful feel no solidarity with the 'welfare clients' and no longer see in their predicament a mirror reflection of their own troubles."[7]

In the end, Bauman comes to acknowledge social life as a wager, a wager where much—and perhaps everything—depends on the ethical commitment of participants. As he insists, a positive answer to the question "Am I my brother's keeper?" cannot rely solely on economic calculations, nor even on psychological dispositions. Reliance on such motivations ultimately is bound to shipwreck on the bedrock of egocentrism or narcissism. The only way to build a viable society is to "open" oneself to the "Other" (as Levinas has taught) and to accept the self's role as a "keeper," guardian, or caretaker of fellow beings. Here Bauman articulates a view of social life which is starkly at odds with the purely "individualized" image invoked in the title of his book. "The human quality of a society," he writes, "ought to be measured by the quality of life of its weakest members. And since the essence of all morality is the responsibility which people take for the humanity of others, this is also the measure of society's ethical standard." As a corollary, this is also the standard by which to judge welfare policies; in fact, it is the "only reason" needed by the welfare state to justify its presence in a "humane and civilized society."[8]

Regimes of Narcissism, Regimes of Despair

For some time, the malaise of egocentrism and narcissism was an affliction troubling chiefly the "West" (meaning Europe and America). Under the impact of Cartesian rationalism and capitalism, Western societies ineluctably underwent the process of disassociation and individuation. But things have changed. Due to the relentless advances of globalization, Western social and psychic dislocations have become worldwide traumas. A telling case in point is India, a country steeped in millennial spiritual traditions and relatively stable social customs. Partly as a result of colonialism and partly of post-independence Westernization, the country underwent powerful winds of change. One of the most astute observers and analysts of these changes is the clinical psychologist and social theorist Ashis Nandy, well known for his books *At the Edge of Psychology* (1990), *Traditions, Tyranny and Utopia* (1987), and *The Intimate Enemy* (1983).[9] When Nandy presented his work as being situated "at the edge of psychology," he made a telling point: in large measure, his writings are a protest against a dominant trend in Western psychology focused on "self-development" or "self-actualization," that is, the assumption that human well-being derives entirely from individual psychic impulses or interests. As a deviant or unorthodox member of the profession, Nandy always explored the close connection between individual, society, and world—including possible dialectical tensions and diremptions.

Seen against this background, Nandy was bound to view the inroads of egocentrism and radical individualism into Indian life as a social pathology, more specifically as a mode of incipient narcissism. Although often touted as a highway to happy self-fulfillment, the pathology to him has the hallmarks of isolation, self-destruction, and despair. This outlook is the gist of his more recent study *Regimes of Narcissism, Regimes of Despair* (2013). One chapter in that book deals with the prevalent utopia of felicity or "happiness," a happiness presumably achieved through self-development and actualization. As Nandy observes, the utopia is basically misdirected and liable to shipwreck if pursued with egocentric means. A "clenched-teeth pursuit of happiness," he writes, has become a "major feature and discovery of our times." In large measure, the pursuit derives its self-confidence from "the power of human volition and the developing technology of human self-engineering as byproducts of the ideology of individualism." These factors prompt many people to believe "that it is up to them, individually, to do something about their own happiness, that happiness cannot happen or occur, nor can it be given: It has to be earned or acquired." Today, this outlook is no longer locally or regionally confined but has become a central plank of a global regime: "the regime of narcissism." In its basic agenda, the regime constitutes a response or rejoinder to a countervailing challenge: "the disease of unhappiness." Unfortunately and predictably, the agenda does not deliver what it promises—thus deepening a sense of lostness or despair. In Nandy's words: "The new global regime of narcissism stands face to face to a new decentralized, fragmented but no less global regime of desperation." That regime is held together not by any single political or social ideology or metaphysics of a good life but by "the widespread experience and psychology of despair."[10]

The effects of desperation are evident in death wishes, suicide epidemics, and more generally a sense of psychic lostness and disarray. In India, this disarray affects especially the large and traditionally stable rural population. Nandy minces no words in depicting the dramatic changes afflicting his country. Here is a gripping passage:

> The suicides of more than two hundred fifty thousand farmers during the last two decades in India . . . tell a story few Indians want to hear. We feel that we have seen enough poverty and suffering over the years to explore how one of the world's most resilient, autonomous, self-confident peasantries is ceding ground to agronomists, laboratories, markets, and the state, and learning to peacefully succumb to despair and self-destruction as its predestined fate.

For the most desperate, self-destruction is the final step; but for them and a multitude of others, the step is preceded by a loss of meaning or purpose—by what Bauman has called the loss of "agency" at the local level. When the farmer's traditional practices are overwhelmed by agronomy and agribusiness, the human quality of farm life is surrendered to the technical heteronomies of profit and efficiency: the earth is no longer cultivated or cared for but exploited for maximal yield. What happens as a result of this change, Nandy notes, is "the destruction of an entire life-support system and way of life, and the consequent loss of [sensible] agency and purpose in life." Applying a broad historical brush, he adds: "The 4,000-year-old peasant lifestyle in India, which till recently constituted the heart of the Indic civilization, is being pushed into extinction."[11]

What is happening to the rural population in general happens with particular vengeance to the multitude of tribal communities and "scheduled castes" (so-called). As Nandy observes, tribal communities and undercastes have emerged as the "underside" or counterfoil of modern or modernizing India. Faced with the relentless advances of mega-technology and the global market, they have been "pushed into destitution, marginalized, and denied even a vestige of dignity." More concretely, they have become the targets of a "double displacement," both external and internal. First, there is the territorial displacement which has turned tribal communities into "floating populations of the disinherited and disposable," and ultimately into the country's "new proletariat." Secondly, tribes have become victims of psychological displacement whereby the distaste for their own "nonmodern" existence and underdevelopment is turned against themselves and against all those who have "lost or opted out of the rat race" of economic and cultural progress. What emerges here is a psychological version of the historical-developmental trajectory. In the view of modern urbanized elites, "tribal India today is what we were yesterday, and their tomorrow is nothing other than what we are today." Built into this trajectory is a stark dichotomy: between winners and losers, victimizers and victims, economic success and despair.[12]

Returning to a theme touched on before, Nandy makes it clear that his argument is not directed against "happiness" per se, and certainly not against Greek *eudaimonia* or the Indian notion of *ananda* (bliss), but only against the narcissistic, "clenched-teeth" counterfeit version. As he observes, this counterfeit version is largely a product of the modern Enlightenment with its confidence in autonomous "human agency, rationality, and individual will." Before that time, happiness tended to be aligned with some form of self-transcendence. The Hindu and Buddhist notion of *ananda* as well as Christian concepts of grace and bliss had little in common with the modern constructivist or engineering variety. Thus, the modern variety associated with individualism and a buffered selfhood had an "uncertain status" in the nonmodern world—even more so, Nandy adds, because some of the older civilizations, such as the Chinese and the Indian, "located their utopias in the past." In the end, Nandy translates the "dialectic of Enlightenment" into a kind of dialectic of happiness where gain and loss, bliss and suffering are intricately entwined.[13]

Pandemic, World Alienation, and Vita Activa

In recent times, the traumas of narcissism and social atomism have descended on large parts of the world in the form of a grim spreading disease: the "pandemic" associated with COVID-19. While initially treated as just an aggravated influenza, the disease soon—at least since the spring of 2020—revealed its real character and scope: the character of a global and potentially lethal and destructive epidemic. The basic remedies marshaled to combat this threat quickly disclosed the disease's radically antisocial or anticommunitarian impact. This is obvious in the two major remedies adopted: the face mask, which inhibits or complicates interhuman speech, and the practice of "social distancing," which militates against social interaction. Thus, as a result of the pandemic, people were thrown ever more deeply into the traumas and agonies affecting contemporary life; as members of atomized and "individualized" societies, they experienced themselves more and more as "noncitizens." To make things worse, governing elites in some countries became increasingly "autistic" and self-enclosed, thus adding to widespread human lostness and desperation.

In the face of these grim calamities, what is clearly called for is a major social renewal. Help in this situation can come from religious resources; but it can also come from philosophical resources, including political thought. As it seems to me, no political thinker is more fitting for the purpose than Hannah Arendt, both in terms of the sharpness of her social and political analysis and her commitment to an active public life. Her major (and justly famous) work in this respect is titled *The Human Condition: A Study of the Central Dilemmas Facing Modern Man*. In that text, Arendt discusses the egocentric malaise under the rubric of "world alienation" or loss of world. Partly in response to Martin Heidegger—who had defined human existence as "being-in-the-world"—she perceived one of the distinctive, dramatic features of modernity in the rupturing of the hyphens linking existence and world. As she writes, very much against the intentions of its early pioneers, the modern age began "by alienating certain strata of the population from the world." Despite a certain nontranscendental or "this-worldly" orientation of the age, this-worldliness in the end ushered in a no-worldliness. What historical evidence shows, she states in an instructive passage,

> is that modern men were not thrown back upon this world but upon themselves. One of the most persistent trends in modern philosophy since Descartes, and perhaps its most original contri-bution to philosophy, has been an exclusive concern with the self, as distinguished from the soul or person or "man" in general, an attempt to reduce all experiences with the world as well as with other human beings, to experiences between man and himself.

The result has been a loss not of self but of world or worldly context: "World alienation, and not self-alienation as Marx thought, has been the hallmark of the modern age."[14]

In her study, Arendt links the loss of worldhood closely with the rise of a purely monetary or capitalist economy in opposition to the earlier agrarian lifestyle. "Expropriation," she writes, "the deprivation of certain groups of their place in the world and their naked exposure to the exigencies of life, created both the original accumulation of wealth and the possibility of transforming this wealth into capital through labor." The new economic system unleashed a vast increase both in productivity and monetary wealth *and* in exploitation or "immiseration." By streamlining everything in the direction of maximum profit, the ordinary lifeworld was stunted; in a strictly antithetical fashion, accumulation thrives only "if world and the very worldliness of man are sacrificed." Arendt's study distinguishes three stages in this antinomian process. The first stage was marked by a sheer "cruelty, misery and material wretchedness," a process meant for the "laboring poor." The second stage was reached when the traditional family life of workers was channeled into harsh economic class structures or nationalist identities. The final stage emerges with the extension and globalization of the market system when "prosperity and depression become world-wide phenomena." Just as, at earlier points, the family and its "property" were replaced by class membership or national identity, so eventually humankind comes to replace nationally bounded society and "the globe replaces limited state territory."

This process of expansion and "deterritorialization" may seem exhilarating to a nomadic, acquisitive mentality, but the cost in terms of alienation is steep: "Whatever the future may bring, the process of world alienation, started by expropriation and characterized by an ever-increasing progress in wealth, can only assume even more radical proportions if it is permitted to follow its own inherent law."[15] For Arendt, one of the most important results of alienation is the loss of a *shared* world, that is, the loss of a "common sense" or common understanding shared by people in a given social context. What takes the place of shared meaning is isolated self-reflection or introspection, which means: reflection not on the deeper meaning of life but on the individual mind and its cognitive operations which are assumed to yield whatever "certainty" can be found. Minding one's own "mind," she notes, is the hallmark of Cartesian rationalism with its focus on *cogito* and *cogitatio* (which always means *cogito me cogitare*). Introspection of this kind promises liberation from external complexities and quandaries because in the mind "man is confronted with nothing and nobody but herself/himself." Arendt quotes Alfred North Whitehead to the effect that Cartesian reason is basically a mathematical reason which, in turn, is "the outcome of common sense in retreat."

This outcome is grave, she adds, because it is "common sense" which once had been the one "by which all other senses . . . were fitted into the common world," but which now has become a purely "inner faculty without any world relationship." To be sure, with this inward turn, "commonality" is not entirely lost; but it is transformed from a common sensibility or understanding into a common rationality, an abstract cognitive condition of possibility. While sense or sensibility in relation to world is plural or multiple, a cognitive condition of possibility is uniform. The rich diversity of world understanding in modernity thus has ceded place to abstract universalism and uniformity. In Arendt's word: "What men *now* have in common is not the 'world' but the structure of their minds, and this they cannot have 'in common' strictly speaking; for their faculty of reasoning can only happen to be the same in everybody."[16]

For Arendt, this transformation and the entire narrative of the dilemmas of "modern man" recounted in her book are deeply disturbing. As a political thinker, her main concern has always been the maintenance of a shared world, and more specifically the maintenance of a public space or "public realm" in which political action can take place. The entire opening section of her study is devoted to the celebration of public agency in a shared world, a world constituted chiefly by intelligible language and mutual interaction. As she writes there: Going on directly between human beings, action "corresponds to the human condition of plurality, to the fact that men, not 'Man,' live on earth and inhabit the world." While all human activities are conditioned by the plural existence of human beings, only public action "cannot even be imagined outside the society of men." Arendt here invokes Aristotle's definition of human being as *zoon politikon* (later translated or mistranslated as *animal sociale*) and continues in a very Aristotelian vein: "Of all the activities necessary and present in human communities only two were deemed to be political and to constitute what Aristotle called the *bios politikos*: namely action (*praxis*) and speech (*lexis*), out of which rises the realm of human affairs."

The combination of speech and public interaction—both seen as "coeval and coequal"—formed the basis of the Greek *polis* viewed as a civic or civilized mode of life: "To be political, to live in a *polis*, meant that everything was decided through words and persuasion and not through force and violence." Against this background, what emerges is a cleavage between ways of life: between a public or civil and a noncivil life, between actions performed in a shared world of meaning and deeds performed outside the range of "common sense" and understanding. With his famous definition, Arendt observes, "Aristotle only formulated the current opinion of the *polis* about man and the political way of life, and according to this opinion, everybody outside the *polis*—slaves and barbarians—was *aneu logos*, deprived (of course) not of the faculty of speech, but of a way of life in which speech and only speech made sense and where the central concern of all citizens was to talk with each other."[17]

Reading this statement together with the previously sketched narrative of the dilemmas of "modern man," one detects a cleavage not only in Greek politics but in the very nature of politics or public life as such. Curiously, Arendt's *The Human Condition* seems to be troubled by a profound tension, perhaps another "dialectic" of modernity—a tension operating between the beginning and the ending of her book. For how is one to reconcile the celebration of public life in the early part of her study with the downward spiral and steady dissolution of "action" in the later parts? As it seems to me, as in the case of Adorno and Nandy, there is no progressive (Hegelian or Marxist) dialectic at work in Arendt's narrative, no dialectical teleology which would usher humanity inexorably forward toward a time of fulfillment. In her discussion of modern rationalism, Arendt refers to the notion of a *deus ex machina*, stating that ultimately "inexplicable goodness is the only thing that saves reality in Descartes' philosophy . . . as it saves the prestabilized harmony between man and world in Leibniz."[18]

Perhaps what makes life livable and preserves hope in the future is again a wager, a trust in a promise or latent possibility. Arendt is well known for stressing the importance of "natality," the argument that every birth brings something new into the world, some kind of openness and novel possibility. Here surely a wager is involved. For what counts is not only the arrival of newness but the cultivation and nurturing of a benign flourishing of human life. This, in turn, depends on the maintenance of a shared world with others in a public space.[19]

8

HOLISM AND PARTICULARISM

Panikkar on Human Rights

The starting point is not the individual but the concatenation of the Real.

—Raimon Panikkar

The notion of "human rights" is a pivotal conception of modern thought, and especially of modern democracy. And clearly, given the experiences of autocracy, despotism, and totalitarianism, the importance of human rights is beyond doubt. Yet, despite the obvious significance of the conception, its meaning and range of application are not easily determined—which has to do in large part with the elusive character of its terms.

The rights in question are called "human," which has a certain intuitive appeal. But what is "human"? Does the term denote a compact entity, with fixed or clearly defined boundaries? Sometimes (or rather most of the time) the rights are called "individual rights," in conformity with the modern penchant to identify "human" and "individual." But again: Does the latter term designate a compact entity with fixed and unalterable contours? And when we turn to the composite expression "human rights," are rights here somehow humanized (which would yield something like "humane rights")? Or is it not rather the common assumption that rights are attached to the "human" like a rightful possession or property? Which means that, in addition to other belongings, like houses or cars, human beings also "own" rights. And when it comes to the notion of "rights," can we assume that their exercise is always rightful or "right"? Hence, what is the rightness of rights? The preceding questions only scratch the surface of the cauldron of issues connected with the conception of human rights. What is clear is that the conception stirs up difficult questions about human nature, justice, and the good life; hence, its discussion can hardly proceed without attention to such fields of inquiry as anthropology, philosophy, and even cosmology. It is commonly acknowledged that the phrase "human rights" arose basically in Western modernity and hence forms part and parcel of a complex constellation of ideas which circumscribes the meaning of "modernity." This constellation differs significantly from the premodern nexus of ideas and life-forms prevailing in (Western) antiquity and the Middle Ages; and it also differs profoundly from many non-Western constellations of thought and conduct. In addition, as many writers have suggested, our contemporary period is marked by a transition between paradigms, bringing into view new horizons of life—including new horizons for the understanding of "human rights."

Hence, the notion (to the extent it is transferrable) occupies a different place in different cultural constellations and cannot simply be transposed intact. All one can do is to look for "equivalences" (provided the differences are not ignored). Moreover, different cultural contexts are not available for neutral inspection; they are not reified pieces in a cultural museum. If paradigms, especially linguistic paradigms, are also "forms of life" (as Ludwig Wittgenstein said), then any move beyond a given paradigm involves an existential agony, a wrenching experience challenging ingrained assumptions and habitual modes of conduct. In the following, I want to explore some of the "wrenching" induced by cross-cultural comparison. In particular, I review arguments advanced by the Catalan Indian thinker Raimon Panikkar about human rights, focusing on his comparison of the modern Western conception with traditional Indian views. By way of conclusion, I explore what character "human rights" might assume in the dawning "post-modern" and post-Western era.

Is "Human Rights" a Western Concept?

Probably the most troubling and frequently debated issue about human rights is whether they are culture specific or at least potentially universal. As it happens, Raimon Panikkar has discussed this issue in an illuminating way some three decades ago in an essay titled "Is the Notion of Human

Rights a Western Concept?" He answers the question ultimately with "yes" and "no," but only after having subjected the notion to close cross-historical and cross-cultural scrutiny. Broadly speaking, one might say that the concept of human rights is one way in which human beings generally articulate the desire for a just social order. "Human rights," Panikkar states, "are *one* window through which one particular culture envisages a just human order for individuals." But, of course, there are other possible approaches, and those who live in a given culture "do not see the window" (or do not see it as a window). Other cultures or historical contexts may use different formulations which are (what he calls) "homeomorphic equivalents" to, though not identical with, human rights. Yet, this very broad and irenic way of looking at things is not how the concept is predominantly used today. In its distinct contemporary usage, the notion of human rights glances definitely through a particular window: that is, modern Western culture, and bears the earmarks of the genesis and unfolding of Western modernity.[1]

To grasp this modern character, historical comparison is helpful. The modern age (so-called) emerged through rupture from a preceding and very different paradigm: a "premodern" paradigm in which human beings and all particular entities were subordinated to, and integrated into, a broader social and cosmological fabric. In Panikkar's words: Western societies have been involved in "a process of transition from more or less mythical *Gemeinschaften* (feudal principalities, self-governing cities, guilds, local communities . . .) to a 'rationally' and 'contractually' organized 'modernity' as known to the Western industrialized world." Differently phrased: Life in the West passes "from a corporate belonging in a community based on practically accepted custom and theoretically acknowledged authority, to a society based on impersonal law and ideally free contract, to the modern state," a passage accompanied by the steady "growth of individualism."

Nowhere is the drama of the passage move evident than in the work of Thomas Hobbes (not mentioned by Panikkar). In a radical move, Hobbes brushed aside the holistic teleology and cosmology of Aristotle and proceeded to disaggregate social wholes into an array of isolated particular individuals struggling for survival in the "state of nature." To human beings in this condition he assigned basic human rights—in effect a "right to everything" (*ius ad omnia*) necessary for their survival. Here the paradigmatic reversal is clear: while previously the "whole" (*omnia*) embraced particulars, the latter were now entitled to appropriate the whole as a proprietary right. This proprietary character came to overshadow and mark the subsequent course of Western "liberalism"—as is manifest in John Locke's formula "life, liberty, and property" (where the former two are likewise natural possessions).[2]

Panikkar's essay lucidly distills the basic "assumptions and implications" of the modern Western paradigm. Focusing on the Universal Declaration of Human Rights of 1948, he notes the "liberal Protestant roots" of that document. Among the guiding ideas of the declaration, he singles out chiefly these features: the assumption of a "universal human nature common to all people," which is knowable through the exercise of reason and which is "essentially different from the rest of [nonhuman] reality"; further, the assumption of the basic "dignity of the individual" irrespective of rank, race, or religion, coupled with the autonomy of that individual vis-à-vis society, nature, and the cosmos; and finally the assumption of an (actual or possible) "democratic social order" where all individuals are equal in rights and where society is the aggregate of individual wills and interests.

Summing up these various assumptions, he finds underlying the declaration the premise (not always consciously embraced by the framers) of "a certain philosophical anthropology or individualist humanism" (often called anthropocentrism and egocentrism). As Panikkar acknowledges, this general premise is contested even within modern Western culture. Thus, we find religious dissenters (who challenge the "naïve optimism" regarding human goodness and autonomy); cultural dissenters (who challenge the cogency of the paradigm based on the rise of multiculturalism); and economic, especially Marxist, dissenters (who treat human rights as a camouflage for class rights and economic privilege). But even in their critical remonstrations, dissenting voices often share basic features of the contested paradigm.[3]

To illustrate the contours of the modern conception of rights, Panikkar turns to the Indian philosophical and religious tradition, as recorded in the Dharmashastras, the Bhagavad Gita, and the great epics. As he points out, the term *dharma* is perhaps "the most fundamental word" in the entire Indian tradition and could conceivably serve as a "homeomorphic equivalent" to human rights. However, the equivalence is undercut or rendered doubtful by the multivalent character of *dharma*—which can mean, in different contexts, things like "law, norm of conduct, right, truth, justice, righteousness," and even religion and cosmic order. To find the common core of these notions, one has to uncover the "root metaphor" of all these meanings—which reveals that the term basically refers to "what maintains, gives cohesion and thus strength to any given thing, to reality, and ultimately to the 'three worlds' (*triloka*)" or the cosmos.

In every case, the emphasis is on keeping together, keeping intact, maintaining order. Thus, *dharma* in its various shadings is "not concerned with finding the 'right' of one individual against another or of the individual vis-à-vis society." In Panikkar's words: "The starting point here is not the individual, but the whole concatenation of the Real." Differently phrased: *Dharma* is "the order of the entire reality, that which keeps the world whole together." To be sure, to maintain this order, individuals and all particular elements have to play their part. Thus, the individual's duty is indeed "to maintain his 'rights'"—but the latter here signifies the task "to find one's place in relation to society, to the cosmos, and to the transcendent world."[4]

At this point, one needs to guard against holistic extremism. The Indian tradition also has the notion of *svadharma*, that is, a *dharma* which is appropriate for the "self" or one's own life. However, even here the equivalence is limited, because the notion cannot be abstracted from the holistic order. In confrontation with the Western model, Panikkar notes, the Indian tradition would critically stress "that human rights should not be absolutized"; it would contest "that one can speak of human rights as 'objective' entities standing on their own in isolation from the rest of the Real." Proceeding on this critical plane, the essay highlights a number of important distinctions. First of all, from the Indian vantage, human rights are "not *individual* rights only." The reason is that, in that tradition, the individual is seen only as a "knot" embedded in a "net" of relationships which form the fabric of reality. Hence, individuality is not a "substantial category." Basically the cosmic structure is "hierarchical"—although this does not mean that "higher echelons have the right to trample upon the rights of lower ones."

Secondly, rights are "not *human* rights only." They mesh with "the entire cosmic display of the universe." Thus, animals, all sentient beings, and even supposedly inanimate beings are all involved in the interaction or correlation of dharmic rights. Finally, human rights are "not *rights* only," because they are also duties and both are interdependent. Thus, taking the core right in the Western model—that of survival or self-preservation—one can say that human beings, in the Indian vision, have the right to survive only insofar as they also perform "the duty of maintaining the world" (*lokasamgraha*). As Panikkar states, "Our right is only a participation in the entire metabolic function of the universe." From this angle, the Declaration of 1948 would need to be amended or rephrased as a "Declaration of Universal Rights and Duties in which the whole of Reality is encompassed."[5]

Panikkar does not claim or pretend that the traditional Indian model can be preserved or reaffirmed intact in our time. He is fully aware of the blemishes and defects of traditional culture as it developed through the centuries, especially the blemishes of untouchability and an increasingly rigid caste structure—defects against which Gandhi, Ambedkar, and many others have struggled so valiantly in recent times. Moreover, he realizes that Western modernity has penetrated Indian culture and society on all levels, bringing with it such changes as urbanization, market economy, and an increasing focus on the rights of individuals and particular groups. As he states clearly, the notion "that the rights of individuals be conditioned by [or dependent on] their position in the net of Reality can no longer be admitted by the contemporary mentality."[6]

There is also a further consideration: Under present-day conditions, clinging to old-style holism can be misleading and even dangerous. In a context steadily marked by Western-style individualism and anthropocentrism, holism is in danger of being perverted into an ideological project manipulated by demagogues or extremist political leaders. The example of "Hindutva" (India for Hindus only) and the excesses associated with Ayodhya are vivid reminders of this possible decay. This does not mean that concern for the "whole" or the "common good" must be completely abandoned, but it does mean that such terms have to be used with utmost caution as a distant horizon and always with full awareness of prevailing differences of perspectives which are precisely not "common."

What emerges from these considerations is the desirability of a midway position, of a simultaneous affirmation and critique of the Western model. Panikkar is emphatic on the needed affirmation, especially in view of the immense dangers to human dignity posed by the rise of modern mega-powers, such as mega-states and mega-corporations. In his words: "For authentic human life to be possible within the *megamachine* of the modern technological world, human rights are imperative. A technological civilization without human rights amounts to the most inhuman situation possible." At the same time, the Western model should not be unduly glorified, for it seems excessive to claim that "the rights of individuals [or groups] be so absolute as not to depend at all on the particular situation or context." To make such a claim conjures up the noted perils of anthropocentrism and egocentrism.

For Panikkar, the sensible position involves negotiation, more specifically a mutual learning process between cultural paradigms or constellations: "A mutual fecundation of cultures is a human imperative of our times." To make such fecundation possible, an "intermediary space" needs to be found which allows for mutual learning, criticism, and transformation. This intermediary space is that of dialogue—what he also calls a "diatopical dialogue" because it involves a movement between different places or contexts (*topoi*). "No culture, tradition, ideology or religion," we read, "can today speak for the whole of humankind, let alone solve its problems. Dialogue and intercourse leading to a mutual fecundation are necessary." To be fruitful, such dialogue has to rely on mutual interpretation, and hence on the resources of a "diatopical hermeneutics" which makes it possible "from the *topos* of one culture to understand the constructs of another."[7]

Panikkar's essay is most helpful and promising for future developments when he turns from a simple opposition of models to some fruits of intercultural fecundation. One such fruit concerns the bearer of human rights. Moving beyond the absolutism of separate individuals (marking the Western model) and the collectivist holism (of tradition), he introduces the notion of the "person" seen as an ensemble of relations. "The person," he writes, "should be distinguished from the individual." While the latter is an abstraction, "my person" calls forth all my correlates: "my parents, children, friends, foes, ancestors and successors"—none of whom can be called my property or accessory. Thus, while an individual is an "isolated knot," a person is "the entire fabric around that knot, woven from the total fabric of the Real."

An equally important fruit has to do with a reformulation of the philosophical character of rights, a reformulation intimating a new correlation of "knot" and "net" or fabric. Basically, he writes, "traditional cultures have stressed the net (the role of each part in relation to the whole), so that often the knot has been suffocated and not allowed sufficient free space." On the other hand, "modernity stresses the knots (individual free will to choose any option), so that often the knot has been lost in loneliness, or else wounded or killed in competition with other more powerful knots." While traditional culture may be termed "cosmocentric" and the modern Western model "anthropocentric," maybe the time has come for a "cosmotheandric vision of reality," where "the divine, the human, and the cosmic" are each given their due, functioning in harmonious cooperation and allowing for "the performance of our truly human rights."[8]

Rights and Right(ness)

The preceding discussion attests to an impending paradigm shift in the area of human rights: a shift from the exclusive focus on the Western model to a more global and ecumenical model of rights. In their basic thrust, the reviewed arguments seek to modify or at least supplement the Western focus on individual self-interest and anthropocentrism with a greater attentiveness to ethical and religious considerations. However, although valuable, this ethical-religious correction by itself may not be sufficient to satisfy universal aspirations. There are other impediments to the universal functioning of human rights. These obstacles have to do mainly with geopolitical, economic, and technological asymmetries. Here, the question raised by Theodor Adorno becomes relevant: How is ethics supposed to function in the general context of a "damaged life," that is, a context where rights and ethical concerns are systematically marginalized?[9] What emerges here is the realization that the question of human rights presupposes the cultivation of a broad context of "rightness" reaching from political to economic and social domains. This might be called the "rightness" frame of rights.

As it happens, contemporary human rights discourse is aware of this need for a broader frame. It is customary in this discourse to distinguish between three "generations" of rights: first, civil and political rights (anchored in modern Western individualism); next, social and economic rights (sponsored chiefly by socialist or socially progressive movements); and finally, cultural and collective rights (championed mainly by non-Western and indigenous peoples). The three generations are by no means in preestablished harmony or easily reconciled. In fact, the dominant Western rights discourse grants almost exclusive preference to the first generation while sidelining, and even accepting the infringement on, second- and third-generation rights. For this reason, the East Asia expert Henry Rosemont Jr. calls the dominant human rights discourse a "bill of worries" concealing or papering over underlying conflicts and inequities.[10]

These inequities have been eloquently highlighted by Chandra Muzaffar in his comments on the three generations: "By equating human rights [solely] with civil and political rights, the rich and powerful people in the North hope to avoid coming to grips with those economic, social and cultural challenges which could well threaten their privileged position in the existing world order. What the rich and powerful do not want, above all, is a struggle for economic transformation presented as a human rights struggle, a struggle for human dignity." These comments are ably seconded by the Indian social theorists Smitu Kothari and Harsh Sethi, in their book *Rethinking Human Rights*, when they charge the Western model with hiding from view the plight of the vast majority of humankind, including the majority of people in their native India.[11] What these critical voices challenge is not so much the importance of civil and political rights per se, as rather their presumed ability to operate in a vacuum separated from social, economic, and cultural aspirations. Viewed from this angle, what the contemporary "Axial Age" brings into view is a new and integrated human rights paradigm where the "generations" of rights would be reconciled on a global level. In the words of Kothari and Sethi, what is demanded in our time is a human rights praxis which is also a "humane" rights praxis inspired by "rightness," that is, "a social praxis, rooted in the need of the most oppressed communities, that aims to create shared norms of civilized existence for all."[12]

As it seems to me, this kind of social praxis was at the heart of the American civil rights struggle led by Martin Luther King Jr., a struggle which aimed not only at securing for African Americans political rights in a narrow sense, but also to foster their economic, social, and cultural freedom and dignity. It was a similar comprehensive vision which guided the Mahatma Gandhi in his struggle for Indian independence where the ouster of British rule was only meant as a preamble to the cultivation of India's flourishing in the political, economic, and cultural domains. To this extent, Martin Luther King, Gandhi, Nelson Mandela (and others) have been pioneers in rekindling in our time the integral sense of humaneness (*jen*), rightness (*dharma*), and justice as guiding motifs for the conduct of human and public life. The point today is not to erect monuments to these pioneers, thus reducing them to museum pieces. Rather, the task is to follow their lead by practicing "rights" in a non-unilateral but interactive and ethically responsible manner oriented toward the "cosmotheandric" or "anthropocosmic" flourishing of humankind.[13]

9

FALLING UPWARD COMMUNALLY

A Tribute to Richard Rohr

> The divine presence seeks connection and communion, not separation
> or division.
>
> —Richard Rohr

Politics is a double-edged practice, combining the best and the worst of human possibilities. In its best moments, politics aims at justice and the ethically "good life," thus honoring or paving the way toward an ideal community. In its worst moments, by contrast, it resembles a fury or raging fire destroying everything in its path. In recent years, the negative or destructive side of politics has steadily moved into the foreground, both in America and the rest of the world. Instead of pursuing justice and the good life for all, political leaders are increasingly committed only to personal or sectarian power over others. In this harsh power game, there are only winners and losers, not citizens in a shared public regime.[1] In recent times, no one has challenged this win-lose paradigm more consistently and more reflectively than the Franciscan priest Richard Rohr, head of the Center for Action and Contemplation in Albuquerque. As the name of the center indicates, Rohr shares with Panikkar and others a "post-secular" outlook, that is, a balanced commitment not just to activism but to social and political reform anchored in spiritual meditation or reflection.

This post-secular perspective is clearly reflected in Rohr's comments on freedom and human rights. In opposition to a purely self-centered and "neo-liberal" conception, the priest articulates a faithful freedom or a "theology of liberation." As he states in some recent meditative messages, the idea of a faithful liberation can be traced back to the Exodus of the Israelites from Egypt—an Exodus which is not a complete withdrawal from the world and its tribulations but the ascent to a new communal spiritual vision free from self-centered aims: "The story of Israel symbolically captures the experience of our own liberation which yields both an outer and (especially) an inner freedom." In this context, Rohr refers specifically to the parallel of the biblical Exodus story and the experience of African Americans who (in the words of Allen Callahan) "have read and retold the story more than any other biblical narrative" as foretelling their own "liberation from bondage." Most importantly, liberation in the biblical sense is not simply an act of private self-liberation, but it is received from a higher source—which, in its liberating move, reveals its own transcendent and undomesticated character. As he points out, God as liberator is "Being itself, Existence itself, a nameless God beyond all names, a formless God previous to all forms, a God who is utterly liberated from the limits culture and religion put on any divinity." This God asserts his "ultimate freedom from human attempts to capture the Divine in concepts."[2]

The Universal Christ

With his stress on the liberating quality of the divine, Rohr clearly takes a stand against any particularist or sectarian appropriation of faith. In this manner, he shows himself as a peacemaker, as one firmly opposed to the win-lose formula or the equation of politics with a raging and destructive fire. To be sure, by emphasizing divine transcendence, Rohr does not mean to reduce faith to a speculative abstraction, far removed from the concrete concerns of the world. Such an outlook would be at odds with the "post-secular" leanings of our time discussed before. Together with Panikkar, the Franciscan champions a nondualist or advaitic position, a view which recognizes difference while upholding a close correlation or symbiosis. Thus, the talk about "a nameless God beyond all names, a formless God behind all forms" should not make us forget the characterization of God as "Existence itself," as the source and essence of all beings in the world. The basic character and implication of this correlation are spelled out in Rohr's celebrated *The Universal Christ*, a text which does not announce a dogma but a new experiential perspective which "can change everything we see, hope for, and believe."[3]

What is hidden behind the book's title is the enigma of the divine-human relationship. Scripturally and theologically this enigma is announced in the expression "Jesus Christ." Since the Great Schism between Eastern and Western churches, Rohr notes, "we (in the West) have gradually limited the divine presence to the single body of Jesus—when that presence is as ubiquitous as light itself, un-circumscribable by human boundaries." With this limitation, we have closed the "door of faith" on the broader and more beautiful understanding of what the early Christians still called the "manifestation," the "epiphany," or simply the "incarnation" of the divine. But the door of faith can be reopened with the key contained in the word *Christ*: "What if Christ is the name for the *transcendent* (being) within everything in the universe? What if Christ refers to an infinite horizon that pulls us from within and pulls us forward too? What if Christ is another name for everything—in its fullness?" What if Christ is the name for the divine source of everything, for the sacred blessing or deep meaning in all things? In this case we discover a new sense of "religion" (which literally means realignment or reconnection). We discover a "cosmic notion" of Christ which "excludes no one but includes everyone and everything," thus allowing Jesus Christ finally to be a "God figure" worthy of the entire universe. In this understanding, Rohr adds, divine love and presence are "grounded in the created world," and the dualist distinction between "natural" and "supernatural" or between world and transcendence sort of falls apart. In any event, we come to see that "Christ is not Jesus's last name."[4]

Throughout his book, Rohr insists on the "universality" of Christ, where that term militates against separation and fragmentation; but he does not ignore the differences of concrete beings. As he writes, "Everything visible, without exception, is the outpouring of God." But he acknowledges that we encounter divine presence "in other human beings" (who are not the same), "in a mountain, a blade of grass, or a starling." Hence, the nondualism Rohr favors is not simply a uniformity or sameness, but a unity of differences or a differentiated unity or nonfragmentation. "My point is this," he writes, "when I know that the world around me is both the hiding place and the revelation of God, I can no longer make a significant distinction between the natural and the supernatural, between the holy and the profane"—and also between me and the other (or a distinction which would amount to opposition or enmity). As he adds: "Everything I see and know is indeed one *uni-verse* revolving around one coherent center. The divine present seeks connection and communion, not separation or division—except for the sake of an even deeper future union."[5] Thus, difference and ontological distinction may have their religious significance in a divine place evolving toward a deepened union or communion. Unfortunately, in recent Western history, difference has been only the engine promoting separation and hostility. Differential wholeness as envisaged in his book is something our present world "no longer enjoys and even vigorously denies." In Rohr's words: "Intellectuals in the last century have rejected the existence and potency of cosmic wholeness, and in Christianity we have made the mistake of limiting the Creator's presence to just one human manifestation, Jesus. The implications of our very selective seeing have been massively destructive for history and humanity. Creation was deemed profane, a pretty accident." This way of seeing "makes us feel separate and competitive, striving to be superior instead of deeply connected, seeking ever larger circles of union."[6]

For Rohr, disunity thus can be a stepping-stone toward greater unity. The same relation holds true (or can hold true) for the opposition between darkness and light and between suffering and joyful deliverance. In the Christian tradition, the most important correlation obtains between the cross and redemption. In this respect, Rohr follows his great Franciscan mentor St. Bonaventure (1221–1274), especially his notion of the "coincidence of opposites" or the close correlation of (seeming) contraries. In ordinary secular life, a close parallel to the cross can be found in genocide or the Holocaust. Rohr at this point refers to Etty Hillesum, a young Jewish woman who was killed at Auschwitz—but who also bore witness to the universal Christ mystery. For, in the midst of misery and destruction she testified to the ultimate goodness and "complete wholeness" of life. In Rohr's words, Etty exemplified a crucial aspect of Christ's voice: "It calls all things to *become whole and true* to themselves," by using the two chief tools of "great love and great suffering." The "supreme irony of life," he adds, is that Christ "*works through* what often seems like un-wholeness and untruth"; thus, "God seems to send us on the path toward our own wholeness not by eliminating the obstacles (of misery), but by making use of them." Rohr also refers to the Swiss psychiatrist Carl Jung who elaborated on what he called a "whole-making instinct" in the human psyche. As a result of a long string of disappointments and tragedies, Jung came to understand "that the full journey towards wholeness must always include the negative experiences (the cross) that we usually reject."[7]

Later in his book, Rohr returns to the notion of nondualism by pondering again the relation between Jesus and the Christ. His reference at this point is to two witnesses after the resurrection: Mary Magdalene and St. Paul. The former "fully knew Jesus in his humanity and was also the first to see him as the Risen Christ," while the latter "never knew Jesus in his humanity and almost entirely speaks of Christ." The two complement each other; they both guide and direct the Christian experience, but "from opposite sides." Mary Magdalene knew the real-life Jesus; according to the gospels, she was his follower and friend. But after the crucifixion a change or transformation happened when the risen Jesus addressed her as "Mary" and her eyes were opened. Thus, Rohr writes, Mary Magdalene "serves as witness to personal love and intimacy," which for most people is "the best and easiest start on the path toward universal love." In the garden after Easter, she experienced "a sudden shift of recognition toward the universal presence of Christ" (who is indeed a "gardener" of souls). By comparison, Paul "starts with the Universal Christ" and then is led to a "deep devotion to the crucified and resurrected Jesus." While traveling on the road to Damascus, Paul—on hearing Jesus's voice—undergoes a radical transformation, from the old sectarian "Adam" to a new liberated seeker. In Rohr's words, going beyond individual aims, Paul realized "that only corporate (communal) goodness could stand up to corporate evil"—thus his emphasis on "community building and 'church.'" Anchoring himself in "Christ," Paul was able to see the normal human situation "as entrapment, even as slavery," and together with Jesus tried "to lead us out of our ephemeral, passing, oppressive, and finally illusory life."[8]

At the end of his study, Rohr adds an appendix which discusses four possible "worldviews," in an effort to pinpoint more clearly his own perspective. One view is called a "material" or materialistic worldview; it has some positive but mostly negative consequences. The view improved living conditions for many people, but in the last couple of centuries it has come to dominate most "developed" countries, creating highly consumer-oriented, competitive, and selfish cultures. Another option is a strictly "spiritual" worldview focused on the "invisible world behind all manifestations." Although uplifting in many ways, this view tends to have "little concern for the earth, the neighbor or justice" because it treats the world simply as an illusion. A third worldview, in Rohr's account, is the "priestly" perspective which tends to be concerned mainly with the law, scriptures, and sacred rituals. Although preserving valuable traditions, champions of this view tend to be dualistic and erect a status difference between clergy and the common people. The view most attractive to the Franciscan is what he calls an "incarnational" worldview, but which might also be called a "nondualistic" or "transformative" outlook. From this perspective, "matter and spirit reveal and manifest each other." The emphasis is "more on awakening than joining, more on seeing (and understanding) than obeying, more on growth of consciousness and love than on clergy, experts, morality, or rituals." The code word for this outlook in Rohr's study is simply "Christ." Most important and most appealing (to Rohr) is the aspect that the fourth outlook combines "prayer with intense social involvement," action and contemplation; it stresses "hands-on" religion and not solely mystical esotericism.[9]

The Divine Dance

The Franciscan priest is not only an incarnational nondualist but also a trinitarian thinker in a transformative sense. This is evident in the study written with Mike Morell, titled *The Divine Dance: The Trinity and Your Transformation* (2016). As Rohr insists in this text, transformation here amounts literally to a "spiritual paradigm shift." He refers in this context to Karl Rahner's famous statement that "Christians are, in their practical life, almost entirely monotheists. We must be willing to admit that, should the doctrine of the Trinity have to be dropped as false, the major part of our religious literature could well remain internally unchanged."[10] Confronted with this traditional Christian "theism," *The Divine Dance* upholds a radically different conception: that the Trinity describes "the very heart of the nature of God." To accept this view, we have to understand that we are not dealing with a triad of separate, static entities but with a transformational flow of three equal partners. In Rohr's words: "Whatever is going on in God is a flow, or radical relatedness, a perfect communion between them—a circle dance of love. And God is not just a dancer, God is the dance itself." To flesh out this image, he cites a spiritual writer of our time: "An infinite current of love streams without ceasing, to and fro, to and fro, gliding from the Father to the Son, and back to the Father, in one timeless happening. This circular current of trinitarian love continues night and day."[11]

Scripturally, the idea of trinity goes back to a story in the Bible (Genesis 18:1–8) where Abraham and Sarah sit at their tent in midday and discover three men standing nearby. Noticing a special aura, Abraham quickly bows to them and asks his wife to prepare a special meal for them to eat. In the tradition, the three men have been regarded as angels or else as three messengers of the divine. In Rohr's words: "Abraham and Sarah seem to see the Holy One in the presence of the three, and their first instinct is one of invitation and hospitality," that is, of readiness for a learning experience. The biblical story has been often treated in literature and also in sacred art, especially in iconography. Rohr refers specifically to the depiction of the trinity by the Russian iconographer Andrei Rublev (fifteenth century). In his picture, Rublev used three primary colors to illustrate three facets of the divine. The color "gold" was used for the "Father," who represents perfection, fullness, wholeness, the ultimate source of all things. The color "blue" was chosen to depict the "human," more precisely "God in Christ taking on the world, taking on humanity." For Rohr, the color indicates the merger of sea and sky, the correlation of spirit and matter, divinity and humanity. Finally, the color "green" represents the "spirit," revealing its "endless fertility and fecundity," the quality of "divine aliveness that makes everything blossom and bloom." Moreover, in the icon, the three figures are not simply separated or isolated, but they interact and point to each other—and even make room for an open space for universal participation.[12]

Basically, for Rohr, the trinity is not just a theological doctrine or dogma; rather, its significance resides in its relevance for and penetration into everyday life experience. This relevance is particularly clear in our own time. In bold terms, *The Divine Dance* articulates the concrete implication of the (so-called) "trinitarian revolution" in our contemporary period marked by a "spiritual paradigm shift." As Rohr writes, "I believe we are precisely at a moment" of radical change: "Instead of the trinity being an abstruse conundrum, it could end up being the answer to the foundational problem of Western civilization. Instead of God being the eternal threatener, we have God as the ultimate participant in everything, both the good and the painful." Thus, the trinitarian revolution reveals God "as *always involved* instead of the in-and-out deity that leaves most of humanity orphaned." The implications of this shift are staggering: "Every impulse, every force toward the future, every loving surge, . . . every ambition for wholeness and holiness" is connected with this change. As the Franciscan adds, in a stirring passage:

> If my instincts are right, this unearthing of trinity cannot come a moment too soon. Because I am convinced that beneath the ugly manifestation of our present evils—political corruption, ecological devastation, warring against one another, hating each other based on race, gender, religion, or sexual orientation—the

greatest dis-ease facing humanity right now is our profound and painful sense of *disconnection*.[13]

Falling Upward

If, in the preceding passage, our "dis-ease" is correctly diagnosed, then is there any hope for the future? Or maybe for hope we might substitute "redemptive confidence." In one of his recent writings Father Rohr introduces us to the mystic Julian of Norwich (1343–1415), and specially to her statement: "First we must fall and then we recover from that fall—and both are the mercy of God." What is implied in this statement is something immense and surprising: namely, that falling or transgression itself has (or can have) a redemptive quality.[14] In his *Falling Upward: A Spirituality for the Two Halves of Life*, Rohr reflects and elaborates on this saying, adding rich insights from developmental psychology. In his presentation, "falling" has a different status in two periods of human life: while in the first or youthful period it signifies simply decay and derailment, in the second stage of maturity falling is balanced with upward movement or a possible discovery of meaning and fulfillment.

Like many or most of Rohr's writings, *Falling Upward* is deeply experiential. As he states in the opening pages of his book: "I am driven to write because after forty years as a Franciscan teacher, I find that many, if not most people and institutions remain stymied in the preoccupations of the first half of life." Basically, the preoccupations at that stage center around selfhood and self-preservation. What people seek to do is "establishing their personal (or superior) identity, creating boundary marks for themselves, and seeking security." For Rohr, these aims are "good to some degree" and perhaps even necessary because they provide a starting point and firm leverage. But the starting gate is not the full story; it is "the raft but not the shore." That there is a further journey beyond we know from the clear and uplifting voices of people who have traveled there and "from the sacred and secular texts that invite us to move on." The invitation often has the character of a "promise of hope"; it issues a summons, not a command to go. In any case, there are "guideposts," exemplary mentors, new kinds of goals and "a few warnings." Rohr's personal hope is that his text can offer some help to travelers along the road, especially at the "crossover points" between the first and second periods of life. These crossover points, he says, usually involve some kind of "necessary suffering," some stumbling over stumbling stones, some lostness and homesickness between our apparent and our "true" spiritual self.[15]

Regarding "necessary suffering," Rohr recalls the stark passage in the gospel of Matthew (16:23–26) which says: "Anyone who wants to save her/his life, must lose it; anyone who loses her/his life will find it." He also quotes the depth psychologist Carl Jung who stated that "so much unnecessary suffering comes into the world because people will not accept the 'legitimate suffering' that comes from being human." Legitimate or necessary suffering derives from the strain that inevitably exists between our self-centered ego and our aspirational or true self, that is, between earthly embodiment and divinization—a strain which inhabits our "incarnational" living. The cited passage in Matthew seems stern and "almost brutal," but it captures well what Rohr and others call the overcoming of "the false self," which is our role, title, and personal image that is largely a creation of our own mind and attachments. It will and must "die" in exact correlation to how much we want to move to the "Real." As the Franciscan adds soberly: the aspirational self is "your substantial self which can be neither gained nor lost by any technique, group affiliation, moral code, or formula whatsoever." Surrendering of the false self or surface identity is "the necessary suffering needed to find 'the pearl of great price' that is always hidden inside the lovely but passing shell."[16]

Regarding lostness and homesickness, Rohr cites a poem by T. S. Eliot saying that, in maturity, "we must be still and still moving into another intensity, for another union, a deeper communion." As he comments, there is a to and fro movement in the stages of human life. The point of sacred stories and secular epics is always "to come back home, after getting the protagonist to leave home in the first place." But the meaning of the term "home" changes: "It points backward to an original hint and taste for union, starting in the body of our mother. And it points forward, urging us toward the realization that this hint or task of union might actually be true." "I want to propose," the Franciscan continues, "that we are both sent and drawn by the same force—which is precisely what Christians mean when they say that the Cosmic Christ is both alpha and omega." This means that our life is inhabited by a lostness and a "desirous dissatisfaction" that both sends and draws us forward. The moving force is usually called "spirit," also "holy spirit," which works largely from within, at "the deepest level of our desiring being." This is why scripture says that "the love of God has been poured into our hearts through the holy spirit" (Romans 5:5), and that "we shall not be left orphaned" (John 14:18). Summarizing his thought at this point, Rohr states: "We are created with a drive and need that sends us looking for our true self, whether we know it or not." Thus, "God creates the very dissatisfaction that only grace and divine love can satisfy." And so, willy-nilly, like Odysseus, "we leave from Ithaca and we come back to Ithaca, but now it is fully home, because all is included and nothing wasted or hated."[17]

At the end of his study, Rohr returns to the basic point of his argument: the discovery of a saving grace in seeming loss. "Most of us," he writes, "tend to think of the second half of life as largely about getting old, dealing with health issues, letting go of our physical abilities," but the whole thesis of his book is exactly the opposite: what looks like falling can be experienced as "falling upward and onward," into a broader and deeper reality. Taken in the sense of a loss of our false, immature ego, falling can lead us into a world of new opportunities: we come to see that "failure and suffering are the great equalizers and levelers among humans." Communities and commitments can form around suffering much more than around "our pride at how wonderful and how superior we are." For Rohr, there is a strange and wonderful communion in real-life human pain, actually much more than in exuberant happiness, which "too often is manufactured and passing."[18]

The question an attentive reader is likely to ask at this point is whether this "falling upward" also applies to social, political, and communal life? Is the dis-ease of "disconnection" mentioned before, the illness of self-seeking and fragmentation which troubles our age, just a passing fancy—or does it also contain a promise of recovery and renewal? Rohr does not directly answer this question. But maybe his answer is contained in his concluding meditation on a poem by Thomas Merton which starts with these lines:

> When in the soul of the serene disciple
> With no more Fathers to imitate
> Poverty is a success,
> It is a small thing to say the roof is gone:
> He has not even a house.[19]

CONCLUDING REMARKS

Whoever exalts himself will be humbled,
but whoever humbles himself will be exalted.

—Matthew 23:12

By way of conclusion, it is fitting to remind readers of the basic theme of this study: the paradigmatic shift occurring in our time in several dimensions. This shift separates "modernity" in its classical sense—captured by Descartes in his *cogito ergo sum*—from various forms of "postism" (post-secularism, post-modernity, post-individualism) whose precise meaning is in a process of exploration. This process is still ongoing and, for this reason, is not purely cognitive or academic but has an existential and participatory character. In this sense, the study exemplifies what Richard Rohr calls the correlation of thinking and doing, knowing and practice, and what he seeks to cultivate in his Center for Action and Contemplation. To this extent, every reader is meant to offer not only cognitive assent or criticism but to undergo a possible existential transformation.

In this respect, it is important to ponder what Father Richard calls the two ages of human life: the age of identity and self-definition, and the age of spiritual openness and compassion. In our present time—which seems to be in the throes of adversity and harsh enmity—it is particularly urgent to embrace his vision of a "true" or higher self which leaves behind the temptations of aggressive self-glorification. I am particularly attracted to Rohr's comments in *The Universal Christ* where he announces the end of imperial religion and the "gradual second coming of Christ." In his words: "Our present highly partisan politics, angry culture wars, and circling of the wagons around white privilege are just the final gasps of the old, dying

123

paradigm. Jesus and Paul both believed this already two thousand years ago."
In a way, both pointed us toward what one may call the "second half of
life: spirituality." The important point today is "that God's heart be made
available and active on earth." Thus, the direct result of a genuine preach-
ing of the gospel is "secularism" (or post-secularism), an active engagement
where "the message has become the mission itself and not just the constant
forming of the (clerical) team."[1]

It so happens that, in America, a possible paradigmatic shift from
turmoil and enmity to civility was occurring just on the day devoted to
the legacy of Martin Luther King Jr. This legacy was commemorated in
many speeches around the country. But one part of this legacy which today
deserves to be particularly upheld is his book titled *Where Do We Go from
Here: Chaos or Community?*, published shortly before his death. The book was
written in a difficult and bitter time. As King wrote: "There is no solution
for the black people through isolation" or separation; instead, he urged them
to "move forward nonviolently, accept disappointment, and cling to hope."
In this spirit, he called his followers "to a higher destiny, to a new plateau
of compassion, to a more noble expression of humanness." His people, he
felt, were well equipped to do this, because "we have been seared in the
flames of suffering"; hence, "we must have a passion for peace born out
of wretchedness and the misery of war." As he added toward the end of
his book: "A genuine revolution of values means in the final analysis that
our loyalties must become ecumenical rather than sectional. Every nation
must now develop an overriding loyalty to humankind as a whole in order
to preserve the best in their individual societies." The biblical call for "an
all-embracing and unconditional love" was not just an empty dream but
has become "an absolute necessity for the survival of man."[2]

King's vision inspired many of his contemporaries, including the black
poet June Jordan who clung to the conviction that "we are the ones we
have been waiting for."[3] More recently, this legacy was upheld by another
young poet, Amanda Gorman, in her "inaugural poem," "The Hill We
Climb," which reads in part:

> We are striving to forge a union with purpose,
> to compose a country committed to all cultures, colors, char-
>   acters, and conditions of man.
>   . . .
> We lay down our arms
> so we can reach out our arms
> to one another.

. . .
If we merge mercy with might,
and might with right,
then love becomes our legacy
and change our children's birthright.[4]

NOTES

Chapter 1. Introduction: Emerging from Multiple Rifts

1. For a discussion of some of the major agonies of our time, see my *Political Life in Dark Times: A Call for Renewal* (Lanham, MD: Lexington Books, 2021).

2. For a broad philosophical discussion of the notion of "difference," as employed here, see my *Horizons of Difference: Engaging with Others* (Notre Dame, IN: University of Notre Dame Press, 2020).

3. As I should add, there is a parallel between "post-secularity" and such notions as "post-modernity" and "post-liberalism" in that there is a shared stress on the correlation of seemingly opposed views. Compare, for example, my *Post-Liberalism: Recovering a Shared World* (New York: Oxford University Press, 2019). I do not use the term "post-modern" in the sense of a cult of randomness or civil disorder.

4. See Jacques Maritain, *Integral Humanism: Temporal and Spiritual Problems of a New Christendom*, trans. Joseph W. Evans (Notre Dame, IN: University of Notre Dame Press, 1979), 93, 119. Compare also my "Continuity and Historical Change: Remembering Jacques Maritain," in *Horizons of Difference*, 27–37.

5. Paul Ricoeur, "Ye Are the Salt of the Earth," in *Political and Social Essays*, ed. David Stewart and Joseph Bien (Athens: Ohio University Press, 1974), 115–117. Compare also my "Religious Freedom: Preserving the Salt of the Earth," in my *In Search of the Good Life: A Pedagogy for Troubled Times* (Lexington: University of Kentucky Press, 2007), 205–219. In this context, it is also good to remember the letter of James (James 1:22, 27): "But be doers of the word, and not hearers only. . . . Religion that is pure and undefiled is this: to visit orphans and windows in their affliction, and to keep oneself unstained from the world."

6. See *Faithful America*, January 8 and January 16, 2021, faithfulamerica.org. Regarding the attempt by the Nazi regime in Germany to co-opt Christian faith, compare, for example, Robert A. Krieg, *Catholic Theologians in Nazi Germany* (New York: Continuum, 2004); and Victoria Barnett, *For the Soul of the People: Protestant Protest against Hitler* (New York: Oxford University Press, 1992).

7. Raimon Panikkar, *The Rhythm of Being: The Gifford Lectures* (Maryknoll, NY: Orbis Books, 2010), 128, 133–135. See also his statement: "Neither monism nor dualism, neither pantheism nor atheism nor theism—correspond to the profound experience of our time. The world, humanity and God . . . are intertwined." *The Silence of God: The Answer of the Buddha* (Maryknoll, NY: Orbis Books, 1989), 12.

8. See my *Small Wonder: Global Power and Its Discontents* (Lanham, MD: Rowman & Littlefield, 2005), 4. As an epigraph for that book I chose the words of the Argentinian writer Hebe de Bonafini: "Our country is different from his. His is the military, money, power, a Ferrari. Ours is the men and women who give their lives for it, the Plaza, life, the Earth."

9. Jean Bethke Elshtain, *Democracy on Trial* (New York: Basic Books, 1995), xii, 12.

10. Ronald Dworkin, *Is Democracy Possible Here? Principles for a New Political Debate* (Princeton, NJ: Princeton University Press, 2006), 1. Dworkin's depiction of American democracy as a "form of war" recalls the argument of the German (semi-fascist) theorist Carl Schmitt, who equated politics in general with warfare or the strife between friends and enemies. See his *The Concept of the Political* (1932), trans. George Schwab (Chicago: University of Chicago Press, 1996). As an antidote, see my *The Promise of Democracy: Political Agency and Transformation* (Albany: State University of New York Press, 2010), and my *Democracy to Come: Politics as Relational Praxis* (New York: Oxford University Press, 2017).

11. Herbert Spencer, *The Man versus the State*, ed. Donald Macrae (Baltimore, MD: Penguin Books, 1965), 174–175.

12. William H. Riker, *Liberalism against Populism: A Confrontation between the Theory of Democracy and the Theory of Social Choice* (Prospective Heights, IL: Waveland Press, 1982), 9–12, 246.

13. Raymond D. Boisvert, *John Dewey: Rethinking Our Time* (Albany: State University of New York Press, 1991), 58.

14. Mohandas K. Gandhi, *Hind Swaraj and Other Writings*, ed. Anthony J. Parel (Cambridge, UK: Cambridge University Press, 1997), 42–43, 67, 73.

15. See Tu Weiming, *Confucian Thought: Selfhood as Creative Transformation* (Albany: State University of New York Press, 1985), 59, 76–78.

16. Christopher Lasch, *The Culture of Narcissism: American Life in an Age of Diminishing Expectation* (1979; New York: Norton, 1991).

17. Zygmunt Bauman, *Liquid Modernity* (Cambridge, UK: Polity Press, 2000), x, 18, 37.

18. Bauman, *The Individualized Society* (Cambridge, UK: Polity Press, 2001), 32, 34–36.

19. Ashis Nandy, *Regimes of Narcissism, Regimes of Despair* (New Delhi: Oxford University Press, 2013), x–xi, 170–178. See also Nandy, *At the Edge of Psychology: Essays on Politics and Culture* (Delhi: Oxford University Press, 1990).

20. See especially my *Return to Nature: An Ecological Counterhistory* (Lexington: University of Kentucky Press, 2011), with the appendix "Ecological Crisis and Human Renewal: A Tribute to Thomas Berry," 155–170. Compare also Dallmayr and Abbas Manoochehri, "Pandemic and Human Lifeworld: A Manifest/Hidden Warfare," *Philosophy and Social Criticism* (2021), https://doi.org/10.1177%2F0191453721991400.

21. Thomas Berry, *Befriending the Earth: A Theology of Reconciliation between Humans and the Earth* (Mystic, CT: Twenty-Third, 1991), 15. See also Berry, *Evening Thoughts: Reflections on the Earth as Sacred Community* (Berkeley: University of California Press, 2006).

22. See Raimon Panikkar, "Is the Notion of Human Rights a Western Concept?," *Diogenes* 20 (1982): 77–78, 79–85. Regarding the importance of dialogue, see my *Dialogue among Civilizations: Some Exemplary Voices* (New York: Palgrave/St. Martin's Press, 2002), and *Being in the World: Dialogue and Cosmopolis* (Lexington: University of Kentucky Press, 2013); also Dallmayr and Abbas Manoochehri, *Civilizational Dialogue and Political Thought: Tehran Papers* (Lanham, MD: Lexington Books, 2007).

23. See Peter C. Phan and Young-chan Ro, eds., *Raimon Panikkar: A Companion to His Life and Thought* (Cambridge, UK: James Clarke, 2018). Compare also Anselm K. Min, *The Solidarity of Others in a Divided World: A Postmodern Theology after Postmodernism* (London: T & T Clark International, 2004).

24. See Richard Rohr, *The Universal Christ: How a Forgotten Reality Can Change Everything We See, Hope For, and Believe* (New York: Convergent Books, 2019). See also Panikkar, *The Unknown Christ of Hinduism: Toward an Ecumenical Christophany* (Maryknoll, NY: Orbis Books, 1981) and his *Christophany: The Fullness of Man* (Maryknoll, NY: Orbis Books, 2004).

25. As Rohr writes: "Whatever is going on in God is a flow, a radical relatedness, a *perfect communion* between Three—a dance of love." See *The Divine Dance: The Trinity and Your Transformation* (New Kensington, PA: Whitaker House, 2016), 27. See also Panikkar, *Trinity and the Religious Experience of Man* (Maryknoll, NY: Orbis Books, 1973).

26. Richard Rohr, *Falling Upward: A Spirituality for the Two Halves of Life* (San Francisco, CA: Jossey-Bass, 2012), xxii.

27. Martin Luther King, Jr., *Where Do We Go from Here: Chaos or Community?* (Boston: Beacon Press, 1968).

Chapter 2. Post-Secularity and (Global) Politics: A Need for Redefinition

1. Gilles Kepel, *The Revenge of God*, trans. Alan Braley (University Park: Pennsylvania State University Press, 1994).

2. This is the development leading from Rawls's *A Theory of Justice* (Cambridge, MA: Harvard University Press, 1971) to *Political Liberalism* (New York: Columbia University Press, 1993).

3. Jürgen Habermas, "An Awareness of What Is Missing," in Habermas et al., *An Awareness of What Is Missing: Faith and Reason in a Post-Secular Age*, trans. Ciaran Cronin (Cambridge, UK: Polity Press, 2008), 16–17. See also Habermas, *Between Naturalism and Religion: Philosophical Essays*, trans. Ciaran Cronin (Cambridge, UK: Polity Press, 2008).

4. "An Awareness of What Is Missing," 20–21.

5. "An Awareness of What Is Missing," 16–17, 22. With this statement, Habermas basically accepts the positivist stage theory (first formulated by Auguste Comte) that history moves from religion to metaphysics and then to (post-metaphysical) science.

6. Jürgen Habermas, " 'The Political': The Rational Meaning of a Questionable Inheritance of Political Theology," in *The Power of Religion in the Public Sphere*, ed. Eduardo Mendieta and Jonathan VanAntwerpen (New York: Columbia University Press, 2011), 25–26. The conference had been held in New York City's Cooper Union in October 2009.

7. On Tertullian see *De praescriptione haereticorum* (Freiburg: Mohr, 1892), esp. chapter 7. The conflict between Athens and Jerusalem was also a central theme in the work of Leo Strauss; see on this point my "Leo Strauss Peregrinus," *Social Research* 61 (1994): 877–906.

8. Gianni Vattimo, *After Christianity*, trans. Luca D'Isanto (New York: Columbia University Press, 2002), 38–39. Compare in this context also Kitaro Nishida's comment: "Just as there is no world without God, there is no God without the world. And as Eckhart said, one sees the true God where even God has been lost." Nishida, *An Inquiry into the Good*, trans. Masao Abe and Christopher Ives (New Haven, CT: Yale University Press, 1990), 168–169. For background, see Emmanuel Levinas, *Of God Who Comes to Mind*, trans. Bettina Bergo (Stanford, CA: Stanford University Press, 1998); Jacques Derrida, *The Gift of Death*, trans. David Wills (Chicago: University of Chicago Press, 1995); Jean-Luc Marion, *Reduction et donation* (Paris: Presses Universitaires de France, 1989); and Dominque Janicaud, "The Theological Turn of French Phenomenology," trans. Bernard G. Prusak, in Janicaud et al., *Phenomenology and the "Theological Turn"* (New York: Fordham University Press, 2000), 16–103.

9. See Hans-Georg Gadamer, "The Universality of the Hermeneutical Problem," in *Philosophical Hermeneutics*, trans. and ed. David E. Linge (Berkeley: University of California Press, 1976), 1–20. In his *Knowledge and Human Interests*, trans. Jeremy J. Shapiro (Boston: Beacon Press, 1971), Habermas had tried to limit hermeneutical understanding to the humanities, while exempting natural science and psychoanalytic self-knowledge from such understanding—a procedure which ignored

"post-empiricist" trends in science as well as the issue of depth hermeneutics. See in this respect my "Borders or Horizons? An Order Debate Revisited," in *Small Wonder: Global Power and Its Discontents* (Lanham, MD: Rowman & Littlefield, 2005), 176–198; and my "Life-World and Critique," in *Between Freiburg and Frankfurt* (Amherst: University of Massachusetts Press, 1991), 13–24.

10. Charles Taylor, "Why We Need a Radical Redefinition of Secularism," in *The Power of Religion in the Public Sphere*, 49–50, 52–53. Giving some concrete examples, Taylor adds (54): "The two most widespread this-worldly philosophies in our contemporary world, utilitarianism and Kantianism, in their different versions, all have points at which they fail to convince honest and unconfused people." Extending this point to the relation between himself and Habermas, he states: "He finds this secure [secular] foundation in a 'discourse ethics,' which I unfortunately find quite unconvincing." What Taylor fails to notice is that his rejection of the "epistemic break" also puts pressure on his own ontological or metaphysical break between transcendence and immanence.

11. See in this context my "Postsecular Faith: Toward a Religion of Service," in *Integral Pluralism: Beyond Culture Wars* (Lexington: University of Kentucky Press, 2010), esp. 80–81.

12. The preceding passages can be read as a subtle commentary on the (much later) doctrine of *sola gratia*.

13. Habermas, "An Awareness of What Is Missing," 19. For a somewhat more helpful text, see Hauke Brunkhorst, *Solidarity: From Civic Friendships to a Global Legal Community*, trans. Jeffrey Flynn (Cambridge, MA: MIT Press, 2005).

14. Taylor, "Why We Need a Radical Redefinition of Secularism," 46, 56.

15. Aristotle, *Nicomachean Ethics*, trans. Terence Irwin (Indianapolis: Hackett, 1985), 14–15 (1097a35–1097b15), 34–35 (1103a31–1103b1). See also Chandra Muzaffer, *Rights, Religion and Reform: Enhancing Human Dignity through Spiritual and Moral Transformation* (London: Routledge Curzon, 2002), 104; and my "Religion and the World: The Quest for Justice and Peace," in *Integral Pluralism*, 85–101.

16. In the gospel of John (4:23–24), Jesus simply says: "But the hour is coming and now is, when the true worshipper will worship the father in spirit and truth, for such the father seeks to worship him. God is spirit, and those who worship him must worship in spirit and truth." For the statement of Armstrong, see http://www.ted.com/speakers/karen_armstrong.html. Her words are distantly echoed by Gadamer when he writes: "Just as health is not known in the same way as a wound or disease, so the holy is perhaps more a way of being than of being believed." See his "Reflections on the Relation of Religion and Science," in *Hermeneutics, Religion, and Ethics*, trans. Joel Weinsheimer (New Haven, CT: Yale University Press, 1999), 127.

17. See in this context Paulo Freire, *Pedagogy of the Heart*, trans. Donaldo Macedo and Alexandre Oliveira (New York: Continuum, 1997); also my "Polis and

Cosmopolis," in *Margins of Political Discourse* (Albany: State University of New York Press, 1989), 1–21, and my *The Promise of Democracy: Political Agency and Transformation* (Albany: State University of New York Press, 2010).

Chapter 3. Post-Secular Faith: Toward a Religion of Service

1. John Dewey, "A Common Faith" (Terry Lectures delivered at Yale University in 1934), in *John Dewey: The Later Works, 1925–1953*, ed. Jo Ann Boydston (Carbondale: Southern Illinois University, 1986), vol. 9, 125–145. In his lectures, Dewey steered a course between theism and non-theism, between Spinozistic naturalism and Emersonian transcendentalism or spiritualism. For a sensitive discussion of Dewey's religiosity, see Steven C. Rockefeller, *John Dewey: Religious Faith and Democratic Humanism* (New York: Columbia University Press, 1991), also his "Dewey's Philosophy of Religious Experience," in *Reading Dewey: Interpretations for a Postmodern Generation*, ed. Larry A. Hickman (Bloomington: Indiana University Press, 1998), 124–148.

2. On the notion "post-secular," compare the comments by Jürgen Habermas: "The expression *post-secular* does not merely acknowledge publicly the functional contribution that religious communities make to the reproduction of desired motives and attitudes. Rather, the public consciousness of post-secular society reflects a normative insight that has consequences for how believing and unbelieving citizens interact with one another politically. In post-secular society, the realization that 'the modernization of public consciousness' takes hold of and reflexively alters religious as well as secular mentalities in staggered phases is gaining acceptance." See his "On the Relations between the Secular Liberal State and Religion," in *Political Theologies: Public Religions in a Post-Secular World*, ed. Hent de Vries and Lawrence E. Sullivan (New York: Fordham University Press, 2006), 258. See also my "Rethinking Secularism—with Raimon Panikkar," in my *Dialogue among Civilizations: Some Exemplary Voices* (New York: Palgrave Macmillan, 2002), 185–200.

3. See Max Weber, "Politics as a Vocation" and "The Social Psychology of the World Religions," in *From Max Weber: Essays in Sociology*, trans. and ed. H. H. Gerth and C. Wright Mills (New York: Oxford University Press, 1958), 78–79, 294–295. I bypass here the issue of "charismatic" legitimacy.

4. William James, *The Varieties of Religious Experience: A Study in Human Nature*, 36th impression (London: Longmans, Green, 1928), v, 2–3, 27–28. As James insisted, religious emotions are ordinary "human" emotions like others (27): "If there were such a thing as inspiration from a higher realm, it might well be that a neurotic temperament would furnish the chief condition of the requisite receptivity."

5. *Varieties of Religious Experience*, 28–29, 31.

6. Charles Taylor, *Varieties of Religion Today: William James Revisited* (Cambridge, MA: Harvard University Press, 2002), 3–5, 7. More recently a revised and

greatly expanded version of his Gifford Lectures was published under the title *A Secular Age* (Cambridge, MA: Belknap Press, 2007). The expanded version, however, does not conflict with the earlier text.

7. Taylor, *Varieties of Religion Today*, 9–11, 13–14. Taylor cites at this point W. K. Clifford, *The Ethics of Belief and Other Essays*, ed. Leslie Stephen and F. Pollock (London: Watts, 1947); and also William James, *The Will to Believe, and Other Essays in Popular Philosophy* (Cambridge, MA: Harvard University Press, 1979). See also Carl Schmitt, *Political Theology: Four Chapters on the Concept of Sovereignty*, trans. George Schwab (Cambridge, MA: MIT Press, 1985).

8. Émile Durkheim, *Les formes élémentaires de la vie religieuse*, 5th ed. (Paris: Presses Universitaires Françaises, 1968); for an English version, see *The Elementary Forms of Religious Life*, trans. Carol Cosman (Oxford: Oxford University Press, 2001).

9. Taylor, *Varieties of Religion Today*, 65–67, 77, 99. See also Ernst Kantorowicz, *The King's Two Bodies* (Princeton, NJ: Princeton University Press, 1997).

10. Taylor, *Varieties of Religion Today*, 93–94, 96.

11. *Varieties of Religion Today*, 111–112, 115–116. As one should note, James's later text *A Pluralistic Universe* corrected to some extent the emphasis of his Gifford Lectures on "individual men in their solitude." See *A Pluralistic Universe* (1909; new impression, New York: Longmans, Green, 1932), and chapter 1 in this volume.

12. Taylor, *Varieties of Religion Today*, 23–24.

13. James L. Heft, ed., *A Catholic Modernity? Charles Taylor's Marianist Award Lecture* (New York: Oxford University Press, 1999), 18–19, 35. For a discussion of this text and other writings by Taylor, compare my "Global Modernization: Toward Different Modernities," in *Dialogue among Civilizations: Some Exemplary Voices*, esp. 97–100.

14. Paul Ricoeur, "Ye Are the Salt of the Earth," in *Political and Social Essays*, ed. David Stewart and Joseph Bien (Athens: Ohio University Press, 1974), 105, 115–117, 123. Compare also my "Religious Freedom: Preserving the Salt of the Earth," in my *In Search of the Good Life: A Pedagogy for Troubled Times* (Lexington: University of Kentucky Press, 2007), 205–219. In one of his late writings, Ricoeur returned to the question of religious faith, placing the emphasis strongly on a religion of service in opposition to a religion of domination. See Ricoeur, *Vivant jusqu'à la mort: Suivi de Fragments* (Paris: Editions du Seuil, 2007), especially 89–91.

15. Compare, for example, Abraham Heschel, "The Theology of Pathos," in *The Prophets* (New York: Harper & Row, 1962), vol. 2, 1–11. The legacy found an intense revival during the Nazi regime. Thus, prior to being executed, Dietrich Bonhoeffer noted that "only a suffering God can help"—which means that Christ helps not by virtue of his omnipotence but by virtue of his suffering. See Bonhoeffer, *Letters and Papers from Prison*, 4th enlarged ed., ed. E. Bethge and trans. R. H. Fuller et al. (London: SCM Press, 1971), 361 (letter of July 16, 1944). Curiously, the philosopher of process Alfred North Whitehead also subscribed to this notion when he wrote: "God is the great companion—the fellow sufferer who understands."

See his *Process and Reality: An Essay in Cosmology* (New York: Macmillan, 1929), 532.

16. Among the proponents of this perspective, Gustavo Gutiérrez is well known for his defense of Bartolomé de Las Casas and his role as "protector of the Indians" against imperial Spain, which then was the embodiment of paleo-Durkheimian ambitions. See Gustavo Gutiérrez, *Las Casas: In Search of the Poor of Jesus Christ*, trans. Robert R. Barr (Maryknoll, NY: Orbis Books, 1993), also his *A Theology of Liberation*, trans. and ed. Sr. Caridad Inda and John Eagleson (Maryknoll, NY: Orbis Books, 1973).

17. John D. Caputo, *The Weakness of God: A Theology of the Event* (Bloomington: Indiana University Press, 2006), 38. As one should note, the turning away from "strong" theology does not mean a retreat into isolated inwardness but implies a call to service in the promised "kingdom" (48): "The kingdom of God is a kingdom of base, ill-born, powerless, despised outsiders who are null and void in the eyes of the world . . . yet precisely for that reason the ones whom God called."

18. Richard Kearney, *The God Who May Be: A Hermeneutics of Religion* (Bloomington: Indiana University Press, 2001), 108. Again, dispossession here does not entail private retreat but a reorientation to the "kingdom" (108): "The kingdom is precisely that which can never be fully possessed in the here and now, but always directs us toward an advent still to come—an alternative site from which to begin afresh." Kearney's reference to "self-emptying" or *kenosis* finds a parallel in Gianni Vattimo's *After Christianity*, where salvation history is linked with a certain "secularization": "If it is the mode in which the weakening of Being realizes itself as the *kenosis* of God, which is the kernel of the history of salvation, secularization shall no longer be conceived of as abandonment of religion but as the paradoxical realization of Being's religious vocation." See his *After Christianity*, trans. Luca D'Isanto (New York: Columbia University Press, 2002), 24. Vattimo also comments on the continued relevance of the "church" or religious community in a "postmodern" setting (9).

19. William James, *A Pluralistic Universe* (1909; new impression, New York: Longmans, Green, 1932), 34.

20. William E. Connolly, *Pluralism* (Durham, NC: Duke University Press, 2005), 70–71, 74.

21. Connolly, *Pluralism*, 48, 59, 64. As he adds (65): "The public ethos of pluralism pursued here, solicits the active cultivation of pluralist virtues by each faith and the negotiation of a positive ethos of engagement between them. I am thereby a proponent of civic virtue. But the public virtues embraced are pluralist virtues." Compare also his "Pluralism and Faith," in de Vries and Sullivan, eds., *Political Theologies*, 278–297.

22. *Pluralism*, 48.

23. Jonathan Sacks, *The Dignity of Difference: How to Avoid the Clash of Civilizations* (London: Continuum, 2002), viii, x–xi. As he adds at another point

(13): "Judaism was the first religion to wrestle with the reality of global dispersion. . . . For almost 2,000 years, scattered throughout the world, they continued to see themselves and be seen by others as a single people—the world's first global people." Compare also my "The Dignity of Difference: A Salute to Jonathan Sacks," in my *Small Wonder: Global Power and Its Discontents* (Lanham, MD: Rowman & Littlefield, 2005), 209–217.

24. Sacks, *Dignity of Difference*, viii, xi, 13, 18–19. Together with George Soros, Sacks challenges the reigning "market fundamentalism," the idea that we can leave the market entirely to its own devices. As he notes (15, 28–29), global capitalism today is "a system of immense power, from which it has become increasingly difficult for nations to dissociate themselves." Although benefiting some segments of the population, its social effects in terms of maldistribution constitute "a scar on the face of humanity." Entering into specifics, Sacks reports that the average North American today consumes "five times more than a Mexican, ten times more than a Chinese, thirty times more than an Indian." While nearly one-fourth of the world's population lives beneath the poverty line, almost one billion people are malnourished and without access to medical care.

25. *Al-Qur'an: A Contemporary Translation*, by Ahmed Ali (Princeton, NJ: Princeton University Press, 1984), 54 (sura 3:31), 537 (sura 90: 13–16). Compare also this hadith: "When the Prophet was asked which form of Islam was best, he replied: 'To feed the people and extend greetings of peace to them—be they of your acquaintance or not.'" See *Words of the Prophet Muhammad: Selections from the Hadith*, ed. Maulana Wahiduddin Khan (Delhi: Al-Risala Books, 1996), 57.

26. See *The Bhagavad Gita*, trans. Juan Mascaró (London: Penguin Books, 1962), 56–58, 62 (book 3:7, 20; book 4:11), and compare *Buddhist Peacework: Creating Cultures of Peace*, ed. David W. Chappell (Boston: Wisdom, 1999).

27. Richard Falk, "A Worldwide Religious Resurgence in an Era of Globalization," in *Religion in International Affairs: The Return from Exile*, ed Fabio Petito and Pavlos Hatzopoulos (New York: Palgrave Macmillan, 2003), 186, 194–195.

28. Falk, "A Worldwide Religious Resurgence," 198–199, 202, 205. I underline "legitimacy" to connect this conclusion with the beginning of the present essay. Compare also his book *Religion and Human Global Governance* (New York: Palgrave, 2001).

Chapter 4. Beyond Secular Modernity: Reflections on Taylor and Panikkar

1. Concerning the "crisis of modernity," compare, for example, Oswald Spengler, *The Decline of the West* (1918; New York: Knopf, 1939); René Guénon, *La crise du monde moderne* (1928), trans. M. Pallis and R. Nicholson, *The Crisis of the Modern World* (London: Luzac, 1962); Romano Guardini, *Das Ende der Neuzeit*

(1950), trans. *The End of the Modern World* (New York: Sheed & Ward, 1956); and Leo Strauss, "The Crisis of Our Time," in *The Predicament of Modern Politics*, ed. Harold J. Spaeth (Detroit, MI: University of Detroit Press, 1964), 41–54. Compare in this context the chapter "Global Modernization: Toward Different Modernities," in my *Dialogue among Civilizations: Some Exemplary Voices* (New York: Palgrave Macmillan, 2002), 85–104.

2. In one of his previous writings, Taylor had distinguished between the "boosters" and the "knockers" of modernity. See his *The Ethics of Authenticity* (Cambridge, MA: Harvard University Press, 1992), 11, 22–23.

3. Charles Taylor, *A Secular Age* (Cambridge, MA: Harvard University Press, 2007), 2–3.

4. Taylor, *Secular Age*, 8–10. The comment on existentialism obviously is tailored to the writings of Albert Camus. Regarding deep ecology, the judgment is modified a few pages later (19) where we read that "there are attempts to reconstruct a non-exclusive humanism on a non-religious basis, which one sees in various forms of deep ecology.

5. *Secular Age*, 13–16.

6. *Secular Age*, 16, 19–20.

7. *Secular Age*, 539–542. In another succinct formulation he states (566): "Modern science, along with the many other facets described—the buffered identity, with its disciplines, modern individualism, with its reliance on instrumental reason and action in secular time—make up the immanent frame. Science, modern individualism, instrumental reason, secular time, all seem proofs of the truth of immanence."

8. *Secular Age*, 543, 547–549, 555–556. Taylor's discussion of the different "frames" or "worlds" is often quite ambiguous—to the point of jeopardizing the distinction itself. Thus, with regard to naturalism we read at one point (548): "Belonging to the earth, the sense of our dark genesis, can also be part of Christian faith, but only when it has broken with certain features of the immanent frame, especially the distinction nature/supernature."

9. See Charles Taylor, *A Catholic Modernity?*, ed. James L. Heft, S.M. (New York: Oxford University Press, 1999), 16–19. Compare also his *Sources of the Self: The Making of the Modern Identity* (Cambridge, MA: Harvard University Press, 1989), and *The Ethics of Authenticity* (Cambridge, MA: Harvard University Press, 1992).

10. At one point, Taylor complains that we have moved "from an era in which religious life was more 'embodied,' where the presence of the sacred could be enacted in ritual into one which is more 'in the mind.'" As a corollary of this move, "official Christianity has gone through what we can call an 'excarnation,' a transfer of embodied, 'enfleshed' forms of religious life, to those which are more 'in the head.'" See Taylor, *Secular Age*, 554.

11. *Secular Age*, 19. In his stress on verticality, Taylor seems to have been influenced by a certain "transcendentalist" strand in French post-modernism, manifest especially in the writings of the later Jacques Derrida (under the influence of

Emmanuel Levinas and his notion of the radically "Other"). For a different, more "open" conception of humanism, compare, for example, Jacques Maritain, *Integral Humanism: Temporal and Spiritual Problems of a New Christendom*, trans. Joseph W. Evans (Notre Dame, IN: University of Notre Dame Press, 1973); and Martin Heidegger, "Letter on Humanism," in *Martin Heidegger: Basic Writings*, ed. David F. Krell (New York: Harper & Row, 1977), 189–242. See also my *For a New and "Other" Humanizing* (Mauritius: Lambert Academic, 2019).

12. Raimon Panikkar, *Worship and Secular Man* (Maryknoll, NY: Orbis Books, 1973), 1–2, 10–13. Compare also the chapter "Rethinking Secularism—With Raimon Panikkar," in my *Dialogue among Civilizations: Some Exemplary Voices* (New York: Palgrave Macmillan, 2002), 185–200.

13. Raimon Panikkar, *The Rhythm of Being: The Gifford Lectures* (Maryknoll, NY: Orbis Books, 2010), xxvi–xxx, xxxii.

14. Panikkar, *Rhythm of Being*, 3–4. As he adds somberly (4): "Today's powers, though more anonymous and more diffused, are quite as cruel and terrible as the worst monsters of history. What good is a merely intellectual denunciation in countries where we can say anything we like because it is bound to remain ineffectual. There is little risk in denouncing provided we do not move a finger."

15. *Rhythm of Being*, 4–5. In this context, Panikkar offers some very instructive asides (5): "Now the foremost way to communicate life is to live it; but this life is neither an exclusively public domain, nor merely private property. Neither withdrawing from the world nor submerging ourselves in it is the responsible human attitude."

16. *Rhythm of Being*, 6–7, 17, 23–24. As he adds (24): One must "constantly be on guard against one of the most insidious dangers that bedevils such endeavors: the totalitarian temptation. My attempt is holistic, not global; I am not offering a system."

17. *Rhythm of Being*, 22, 32–33. As the text adds a bit later (51): "Being is not a thing. There is nothing 'outside' Being. Hence, the Rhythm of Being can only express the rhythm that Being itself *is*." For Heidegger's formulations, see his "Letter on Humanism," in *Martin Heidegger: Basic Writings*, ed. David F. Krell (New York: Harper & Row, 1977), esp. 235–236; and *What Is Called Thinking?* [rather: What Calls for Thinking?], trans. Fred D. Wieck and J. Gleen Gray (New York: Harper & Row, 1968).

18. *Rhythm of Being*, 34–35.

19. *Rhythm of Being*, 10, 36, 38–39, 42. Somewhat later (52) the text adds: "Rhythm is a *meta-transcendental* quality—that is, a property that belongs to every being as Being. Rhythm adds nothing to Being, but only expresses a property of Being qua Being. If truth is considered as transcendental because it expresses Being as intelligible, that is, in relation to the intellect, rhythm belongs to Being considered not in relation to the intelligence or the will, but in relation to its totality [or Whole]." This view is said to be also in accord with "the *advaitic* vision of the Rhythm of Being."

20. *Rhythm of Being*, 110, 128, 133–135. In an intriguing aside he adds (135): "The hypothesis I would advance is that Western, mainly Christian and later Muslim monotheism, is a blend of biblical monotheism and the Hellenic mind represented mainly by Plotinus. . . . Neither Plato nor Aristotle . . . was a strict monotheist." For a critique of (imperial-style) political theology, see the chapter "The Secular and the Sacred: Whither Political Theology?," in my *Integral Pluralism: Beyond Culture Wars* (Lexington: University of Kentucky Press, 2010), 45–66.

21. *Rhythm of Being*, 171–172, 174, 179 216, 230.

22. *Rhythm of Being*, 350–351, 359. As he asks dramatically (358): "Who or what will put a halt to the lethal course of technocracy? More concretely: who will control armaments, polluting industries, cancerous consumerism, and the like? Who will put an end to the unbridled tyranny of money?"

23. *Rhythm of Being*, 270–271; Taylor, *Secular Age*, 15–17, 19.

24. *Secular Age*, 17–18. In the same context, Taylor makes some references to Buddhism—which, likewise, remain ambivalent and deeply contestable.

25. Fred Dallmayr, *Small Wonder: Global Power and Its Discontents* (Lanham, MD: Rowman & Littlefield, 2005), 4. See also Arundhati Roy, *The God of Small Things* (New York: Random House, 1997).

26. This is a free translation of Hölderlin's lines: "Wo aber Gefahr ist, wächst das Rettende auch." See Friedrich Hölderlin, "Patmos," in *Poems and Fragments*, trans. Michael Hamburger (Ann Arbor: University of Michigan Press, 1966), 462–463. Compare in this context Maurice Merleau-Ponty, *The Visible and the Invisible, Followed by Working Notes*, ed. Claude Lefort, trans. Alphonso Lingis (Evanston, IL: Northwestern University Press, 1968), also his "Cézanne's Doubt," in *Sense and Non-Sense*, trans. Hubert L. and Patricia A. Dreyfus (Evanston: IL: Northwestern University Press, 1964), 9–25.

Chapter 5. "Man against the State": Self-Interest and Civil Resistance

1. Friedrich Nietzsche, *Thus Spoke Zarathustra*, in *The Portable Nietzsche*, ed. Walter Kaufmann (New York: Viking Press, 1968),160–163. The phrase "specialists without spirit" was used by Max Weber in "Die Protestantische Ethik und der Geist des Kapitalimus," in *Gesammelte Aufsätze zur Religionssoziologie*, vol. 1 (Tübingen: Mohr, 1988), 204. Compare in the preceding context George Orwell, *1984: A Novel* (New York: New American Library, 1943); and Virgil Gheorghiu, *The Twenty-Fifth Hour*, trans. Rita Elden (New York: Knopf, 1950).

2. *Portable Nietzsche*, 160, 162, 174.

3. For some of Spencer's major works, see: *Social Statics* (1851; London: Schalkenbach Foundation, 1970); *Essays: Moral, Political and Speculative* (3 vols., 1868–1874; London: Williams and Norgate, 1901); *The Study of Sociology* (1873;

Ann Arbor: University of Michigan Press, 1969); *The Principles of Ethics* (2 vols., 1879–1893; Indianapolis: Liberty Classics, 1978); *The Principles of Sociology* (3 vols., 1876–1896; New York: Appleton, 1903).

4. Herbert Spencer, *The Man versus the State*, ed. Donald Macrae (Baltimore, MD: Penguin Books, 1969), 148, 174–175.

5. Spencer, *Man versus the State*, 164, 173, 176–177.

6. See, for example, Richard Hofstadter, *Social Darwinism in American Thought* (Boston: Beacon Press, 1955); also Raymond Williams, "Social Darwinism," in *Herbert Spencer: Critical Assessments*, ed. John Offer (New York: Routledge, 2000), 186–199.

7. Spencer, *Man versus the State*, 181.

8. William Graham Sumner, *What Social Classes Owe to Each Other* (New York: Harper & Row, 1883). Compare also Stow Persons, ed., *Social Darwinism: Selected Essays of William Graham Sumner* (Englewood Cliffs, NJ: Prentice Hall, 1969). One of the prominent later heirs of Spencer and Sumner is the Russian American writer Ayn Rand, whose writings have exerted a major influence in recent times on American ("Tea Party") libertarians.

9. Ludwig von Mises, *Human Action* (New Haven, CT: Yale University Press, 1949), 840. The Ludwig von Mises Institute, established in 1982 in Auburn, Alabama, is strongly under the influence of Spencer's *Man versus the State*. For additional discussion of the Austrian School, see chapter 7 in this volume.

10. See Henry David Thoreau, "Essay on Civil Disobedience," in *The Portable Thoreau*, ed. Carl Bode (New York: Penguin Books, 1975), 109–110.

11. *Portable Thoreau*, 111.

12. *Portable Thoreau*, 112–113.

13. *Portable Thoreau*, 113, 119–120, 122, 136.

14. See Erik H. Erikson, *Gandhi's Truth: On the Origin of Militant Nonviolence* (New York: Norton, 1993), 397. For Erikson, the ethical-spiritual motif of *satyagraha* is missed in many translations, such as "passive resistance," "nonviolent resistance," and "militant nonviolence."

15. Mahatma Gandhi, *Satyagraha* (Ahmedabad: Navajivan, 1958), 6. Compare also Indira Rothermund, "Gandhi's *Satyagraha* and Hindu Thought," in *Political Thought in Modern India*, ed. Thomas Pantham and Kenneth L. Deutsch (New Delhi: Sage, 1986), 297–306; also my "*Satyagraha*: Gandhi's Truth Revisited," in *Alternative Visions: Paths in the Global Village* (Lanham, MD: Rowman & Littlefield, 1998), 105–121.

16. Mahatma Gandhi, *India's Case for Swaraj* (Ahmedabad: Yeshanand, 1932), 369. See also Thomas Pantham, "Beyond Liberal Democracy: Thinking with Mahatma Gandhi," in Pantham and Deutsch, eds., *Political Thought in Modern India*, 340–341.

17. Albert Camus, *The Rebel: An Essay of Man in Revolt*, trans. Anthony Bower (New York: Vintage Books, 1956), 6–8. As Camus adds in an existentialist vein (showing the influence of Heidegger, Jean-Paul Sartre, and others): "Man is the only creature who refuses to be what he is. The problem is to know whether

this refusal can only lead to the destruction of himself and of others, whether all rebellion must end in the justification of universal murder" (11).

18. Camus, *Rebel*, 15–17, 22.

19. As one might say, the striving for "a technological world empire" is animated by a "religion of secular mastery." The striving emulates God's omniscience and omnipotence—while completely sidelining divine benevolence, grace, and charity.

20. *Rebel*, 175, 180, 249–251.

21. *Rebel*, 281, 283–285. Camus's arguments proceed from a secular-humanist perspective; but many of his views could also be stated in Christian religious terms, as was done by Gabriel Marcel in his *Man against Mass Society* (first published in 1952, one year after Camus's book). As Marcel states there: "It would be necessary to show that the idea of being creative [or free] always implies the idea of being open toward others: that openness I have called intersubjectivity. . . . The freedom which we have to defend is not the freedom of Prometheus defying Jupiter; it is not the freedom of a being who would exist or would claim to exist *by himself.* . . . Freedom is nothing unless, in a spirit of complete humility, it recognizes that it has a vital connection with grace" (extended to all). See Marcel, *Man against Mass Society*, trans. G. S. Fraser (Chicago: Regnery, 1962), 24, 247.

22. "The Apology," in *Great Dialogues of Plato*, ed. Eric H. Warmington and Philip G. Rouse, trans. W. H. D. Rouse (New York: New American Library, 1956), 437 (32A). As he adds: "It is necessary that one who really and truly fights for the right, if he is to survive even for a short time, shall act as a private man, not as a public man." Perhaps this comment can be read as counseling not a retreat into individual privacy but an engagement in "civil society" (to use the modern term).

23. "Criton," in Warmington and Rouse, eds., *Great Dialogues of Plato*, 454 (49 B). The dialogue puts these words into the mouth of the "Laws": "As things are, if you depart from this life, you will depart wronged not by us, the Laws [the idea of justice], but by human beings only" (459, 54 E).

24. See in this context, for example, Peter Hoffmann, *German Resistance to Hitler* (Cambridge, MA: Harvard University Press, 1988) and *The Second World War: German Society and Resistance to Hitler* (Cambridge, UK: Cambridge University Press, 1994); Gerd Wunder, *Die Schenken von Stauffenberg* (Stuttgart: Müller and Graeff, 1972).

25. See my *The Legacy of the Barmen Declaration: Politics and the Kingdom* (Lanham, MD: Lexington Books, 2019); also Robert A. Krieg, *Catholic Theologians in Nazi Germany* (New York: Continuum, 2004). The people and clergy co-opted by the Nazi regime were called "German Christians" (Deutsche Christen).

26. Dietrich Bonhoeffer, "Ethics," in *Dietrich Bonhoeffer Works*, vol. 6, ed. Clifford Green, trans. Reinhard Krauss, Douglas W. Scott, and Charles C. West (Minneapolis: Fortress Press, 2005), 244. Compare also his "Letters and Papers from Prison," in *Dietrich Bonhoeffer Works*, vol. 8, ed. John W. de Gruchy, trans. Isabel Best et al. (Minneapolis: Fortress Press, 2010). See also his "Thy Kingdom

Come: The Prayer for God's Kingdom on Earth," in my *Legacy of the Barmen Declaration*, 101–115.

27. Camus, *Rebel*, 279. And he adds: "Between two holocausts, scaffolds are installed in underground caverns where executioners celebrate their new cult of silence. What cry would ever trouble them?"

28. *Portable Nietzsche*, 72.

Chapter 6. Neo-Liberalism and Its Critics: Voices from East and West

1. Raymond D. Boisvert, *John Dewey: Rethinking Our Time* (Albany: State University of New York Press, 1998), 51–52. Compare also Isaiah Berlin, *Four Essays on Liberty* (London: Oxford University Press, 1977); and for a critique Charles Taylor, "What's Wrong with Negative Liberty?," in *The Idea of Freedom: Essays in Honour of Isaiah Berlin*, ed. Alan Ryan (Oxford: Oxford University Press, 1979), 175–193.

2. See Robert A. Dahl, *A Preface to Democratic Theory* (Chicago: University of Chicago Press, 1956), 2, 18–19. To Dahl's credit, one has to acknowledge that he stressed not only formal procedural limits but also "inherent social checks and balances." He also refers (22, 82–83) to an "underlying consensus on policy" existing "prior to politics." But the origin of this consensus is not disclosed.

3. Giovanni Sartori, *The Theory of Democracy Revisited* (Chatham, NJ: Chatham House, 1987), vol. 1, 12–13, 17–18, 241–242; vol. 2, 476–477.

4. William H. Riker, *Liberalism against Populism: A Confrontation Between the Theory of Democracy and the Theory of Social Choice* (Prospect Heights, IL: Waveland Press, 1982), 1–3.

5. Riker, *Liberalism against Populism*, 7, 9–12, 246.

6. See Boisvert, *John Dewey*, 58. Compare also Jo Ann Boydston, ed., *John Dewey: The Later Works, 1925–1953* (Carbondale: Southern Illinois University Press, 1981–90), vol. 2, 328; and John Winthrop, "A Model of Christian Charity" (1630), in *Individualism and Commitment in America Life*, ed. Robert Bellah et al. (New York: Harper & Row, 1987), 21–27.

7. Mohandas K. Gandhi, *Hind Swaraj and Other Writings*, ed. Anthony J. Parel (Cambridge: Cambridge University Press, 1997), 30–37.

8. Gandhi, *Hind Swaraj*, 42–43, 67, 73.

9. These and similar statements are collected in the "Supplementary Writings" attached by Parel to his edition of *Hind Swaraj*, 149–150, 171, 185. The sources can be found in *The Collected Works of Mahatma Gandhi* (New Delhi: Government of India, 1958–1989), vol. 75, 146–147; vol. 76, 339–401; vol. 81, 319–321. By "their poets and teachers" Gandhi seems to refer to some of his favorite Western authors like Thoreau, Ruskin, and Tolstoy.

10. See "Supplementary Writings" in *Hind Swaraj*, 155, 189. Taken from *The Collected Works of Mahatma Gandhi*, vol. 85, 32–33, and Jawaharlal Nehru, *A Bunch of Old Letters* (London: Asia, 1958), 512.

11. Ramashray Roy, *Self and Society: A Study in Gandhian Thought* (New Delhi: Sage, 1984), 78. A similar point is made by Bhikhu Parekh in his stellar text *Gandhi* (Oxford: Oxford University Press, 1997), 75–76: "For Gandhi *swaraj* referred to a state of affairs in which individuals were morally in control of themselves and ran their lives in such a way that they needed no external coercion. For Gandhi, *swaraj* thus presupposed self-discipline, self-restraint, a sense of mutual responsibility, the disposition neither to dominate nor be dominated by others, and a sense of *dharma*."

12. Roy, *Self and Society*, 63, 189–190. The possibility of a transformative freedom was actually acknowledged by Isaiah Berlin, but he confined this mode narrowly to mystical or ascetic lifestyles—a confinement aptly criticized by Roy (186–187).

13. Ronald J. Terchek, "Gandhi and Democratic Theory," in *Political Thought in Modern India*, ed. Thomas Pantham and Kenneth L. Deutsch (New Delhi: Sage, 1986), 308. The citation is from M. K. Gandhi, ed., *Non-Violence in Peace and War*, vol. 1 (Ahmedabad: Navajivan, 1948), 269.

14. Terchek, "Gandhi and Democratic Theory," 309, 312. See also Ronald Duncan, *Selected Writings of Mahatma Gandhi* (Boston: Beacon Press, 1951), 78–79.

15. Tu Weiming, *Confucian Thought: Selfhood as Creative Transformation* (Albany: State University of New York Press, 1985), 59, 76–77. Regarding transformative freedom, he adds (78), in a passage critical of modern Western liberalism: "Historically, the emergence of individualism as a motivating force in Western society may have been intertwined with highly particularized political, economic, ethical, and religious traditions. It seems reasonable that one cannot endorse an insight into the self as a basis for equality and liberty without accepting Locke's idea of private property, Adam Smith's and Hobbes's idea of private interest, John Stuart Mill's idea of privacy, Kierkegaard's idea of loneliness, or the early Sartre's idea of [radical] freedom."

16. Tu, *Confucian Thought*, 175.

17. See Tu Weiming, "The Creative Tension between *Jen* and *Li*," in his *Humanity and Self-Cultivation: Essays in Confucian Thought* (Berkeley: Asian Humanities Press, 1979), 6; also Confucius, *The Analects*, 12:1. Regarding the relation between Confucianism and pragmatism, compare David L. Hall and Roger T. Ames, *Thinking Through Confucius* (Albany: State University of New York Press, 1987), 15: "If contemporary comparative philosophic activity is any indication, it might be the pragmatic philosophies associated with Peirce, James, Dewey, and Mead, and extended toward process philosophy such as that of A. N. Whitehead, that can serve as the best resource for philosophical concepts and doctrines permitting responsible access to Confucius' thought."

18. Ni Peinim, "Confucianism and Democracy: Water and Fire? Water and Oil? Or Water and Fish? In Defense of Henry Rosemont's View," in *Polishing the Chinese Mirror: Essays in Honor of Henry Rosemont, Jr.*, ed. Marthe Chandler and Ronnie Littlejohn (New York: Global Scholarly, 2008), 90.

19. William Theodore de Bary, *The Trouble with Confucianism* (Cambridge, MA: Harvard University Press, 1991), 103–108.

20. Liu Shu-hsien, "From the People-as-the-Root to Democracy" (in Chinese); quoted from Ni, "Confucianism and Democracy," 99.

21. Henry Rosemont Jr., *A Chinese Mirror: Moral Reflections on Political Economy and Society* (La Salle, IL: Open Court, 1991), 93.

22. Rosemont, *A Chinese Mirror*, 93; see also his "Whose Rights? Which Democracy?," in *Confucianism and Liberalism* (Beijing: Sanlian Shudian, 2001), section 5 (in Chinese). I am following here Ni Peinim's account in his "Confucianism and Democracy," 93–94.

23. See Christopher S. Queen and Sallie B. King, eds., *Engaged Buddhism: Buddhist Liberation Movements in Asia* (Albany: State University of New York Press, 1996). Among the most notable "engaged" Buddhists are Thich Nhat Hanh, Buddhadasa Bhikkhu, Sulak Sivaraksa, and the Dalai Lama.

24. Abdolkarim Soroush, *Reason, Freedom, and Democracy in Islam: Essential Writings of Abdolkarim Soroush*, trans. and ed. Mahmud Sadri and Ahmad Sadri (New York: Oxford University Press, 2000), 99, 103. See also Muhammad Iqbal, *The Reconstruction of Religious Thought in Islam* (Lahore: Ashraf, 1971); Abdulaziz A. Sachedina, *The Islamic Roots of Democratic Pluralism* (New York: Oxford University Press, 2001); Khaled Abou El Fadl, *Islam and the Challenge of Democracy* (Princeton: Princeton University Press, 2004); M. A. Muqtedar Khan, ed., *Islamic Democratic Discourse* (Lanham, MD: Lexington Books, 2006); Lahouari Addi, *Islam et démocratie* (Paris: Seuil, 2003); John L. Esposito, *Islam and Democracy* (New York: Oxford University Press, 1996); Timothy D. Sisk, *Islam and Democracy: Religion, Politics, and Power in the Middle East* (Washington, DC: United States Institute of Peace Press, 1992); and Richard W. Bulliet, ed., *Under Siege: Islam and Democracy* (New York: Columbia University Press, 1994).

25. Michael J. Sandel, *Public Philosophy: Essays on Morality and Politics* (Cambridge, MA: Harvard University Press, 2005), 9–11, 27, 33.

26. Walter Lippmann, *The Good Society* (1936; New York: Grosset & Dunlap, 1943), 194, 237, 346–347. See also my introduction to *In Search of the Good Life: A Pedagogy for Troubled Times* (Lexington: University of Kentucky Press, 2007), 2–8.

27. Boisvert, *John Dewey*, 68.

28. Dewey, "Democracy Is Radical" (1937), in *John Dewey: The Later Works, 1925–1953*, vol. 11, 298; and "Reconstruction in Philosophy" (1920), in *John Dewey: The Middle Works, 1899–1924*, ed. Jo Ann Boydston (Carbondale: Southern Illinois University, 1981), vol. 12, 186.

29. Dewey, "Creative Democracy—The Task Before Us" (1939), in *John Dewey: The Later Works, 1925–1953*, vol. 14, 228.

Chapter 7. Individualized Life: The Plight of Narcissism

1. See Max Horkheimer and Theodor W. Adorno, *Dialektik der Aufklärung* (New York: Social Studies Association, 1944; new edition: Frankfurt: Fisher Verlag, 1969); *Dialectic of Enlightenment*, trans. John Cumming (New York: Seabury Press, 1972); also my "The Underside of Modernity: Adorno, Heidegger, and Dussel," *Constellations* 11 (2004): 102–120, and "Adorno and Heidegger," *Diacritics* 19 (1989): 82–100.

2. See Sir Henry Sumner Maine, *Ancient Law: Its Connection with the Early History of Society and Its Relation to Modern Ideas* (Boston: Beacon Press, 1963); Ferdinand Tönnies, *Community and Society (Gemeinschaft und Gesellschaft)* (New York: Harper & Row, 1963).

3. Christopher Lasch, *The Culture of Narcissism: American Life in an Age of Diminishing Expectation* (1979; New York: Norton, 1991).

4. Zygmunt Bauman, *Liquid Modernity* (Cambridge: Polity Press, 2000), x, 18, 37.

5. Bauman, *The Individualized Society* (Cambridge: Polity Press, 2001), 32, 34, 36. See also Pierre Bourdieu, "La précarité est aujourd'hui partout," in *Centre-feux* (Paris: Liber-Raisons d'Agir, 1998), 96–97.

6. Bauman, *Individualized Society*, 46, 48–50. See also Joel Roman, *La democratie des individus* (Paris: Calman-Lévy, 1998).

7. Bauman, *Individualized Society*, 72, 74, 76. See also Emmanuel Levinas, *Ethics and Infinity*, trans. Richard A. Cohen (Pittsburgh, PA: Duquesne University Press, 1985).

8. Bauman, *Individualized Society*, 78–79, 81. The wager contained in the welfare state is clearly expressed in this passage (81): "The future of the welfare state, one of the greatest gains of humanity and achievements of civilized society, lies on the front-line of the ethical crusade. That crusade might be lost—all wars involve the risk of defeat. Without it, however, no efforts stand a chance of success. Rational arguments [alone] won't help." Compare in this context also Zygmunt Bauman, *Socialism: The Active Utopia* (New York: Routledge, 2010), where socialism—despite its defective implementation—is presented as a concrete "utopia" and a viable "counterculture" to the exploitative character of capitalism.

9. See Ashis Nandy, *At the Edge of Psychology: Essays in Politics and Culture* (Delhi: Oxford University Press, 1990), *The Intimate Enemy: Loss and Recovery of Self under Colonialism* (Delhi: Oxford University Press, 1983); *Traditions, Tyranny and Utopia: Essays in the Politics of Awareness* (Delhi: Oxford University Press, 1987).

10. Ashis Nandy, *Regimes of Narcissism, Regimes of Despair* (New Delhi: Oxford University Press, 2013), 176, 178.

11. Nandy, *Regimes of Narcissism, Regimes of Despair*, x.

12. *Regimes of Narcissism, Regimes of Despair*, xi.

13. *Regimes of Narcissism, Regimes of Despair*, 180, 186–187.

14. Hannah Arendt, *The Human Condition: A Study of the Central Dilemmas Facing Modern Man* (Chicago: University of Chicago Press, 1958), 230.

15. Arendt, *Human Condition*, 231–233.

16. *Human Condition*, 254, 256–257. See also Alfred N. Whitehead, *The Concept of Nature* (1920; Cambridge, UK: Cambridge University Press, 1955), 32.

17. Arendt, *Human Condition*, 9, 24–27. Despite her invocation of Aristotle in these passages, Arendt otherwise remained distant from him, largely on the (mistaken) assumption that the Stagirite was basically a philosopher of "contemplation" and not action.

18. *Human Condition*, 256.

19. As she writes on "natality": "If action as beginning corresponds to the fact of birth, if it is the actualization of the human condition of natality, then speech corresponds to the fact of distinctness and is the articulation of the human condition of plurality, that is, of living as a distinct and unique being among equals." See *Human Condition*, 158. For a more detailed discussion of Arendt's work, see my "Action in the Public Realm: Arendt between Past and Future," in my *The Promise of Democracy: Public Agency and Transformation* (Albany: State University of New York Press, 2010), 83–97. More generally, on the problem of world alienation, see my *Democracy to Come: Politics as Relational Praxis* (New York: Oxford University Press, 2017), also my *Twilight of Subjectivity: Contributions to a Post-Individualistic Theory of Politics* (Amherst: University of Massachusetts Press, 1981), *Polis and Praxis: Exercises in Contemporary Political Theory* (Cambridge, MA: MIT Press, 1984), and *Language and Politics: Why Does Language Matter to Political Philosophy?* (Notre Dame, IN: University of Notre Dame Press, 1984).

Chapter 8. Holism and Particularism: Panikkar on Human Rights

1. See Raimon Panikkar, "Is the Notion of Human Rights a Western Concept?" *Diogenes* 120 (1982): 77–78. The essay is an expanded and revised version of his presentation at the Entretiens de Dakar in Senegal, 1982. The meeting in Senegal was preceded by a UNESCO symposium held in Bangkok, Thailand, in December 1979, under the title Meeting of Experts on the Place of Human Rights in Cultural and Religious Traditions; see *Final Report*, SS-79/CONF. 607/10 of February 6, 1980.

2. Panikkar, "Is the Notion," 80, 88. For Hobbes's formula, see *Leviathan* (London: Dent & Sons, 1953), part 1, chapter 14, 73; for Locke's formula, see *Two Treatises of Civil Government* (London: Dent & Sons, 1953), book 2, chapter 2, 119.

3. Panikkar, "Is the Notion," 79–85.

4. "Is the Notion," 95–96.

5. "Is the Notion," 97–99. A similar notion of self-preservation can also be found in the philosophy of Spinoza (in contradistinction to that of Hobbes). See in this context my "Nature and Divine Substance: Spinoza," in *Return to Nature? An Ecological Counterhistory* (Lexington: University of Kentucky Press, 2011), 11–32.

6. "Is the Notion," 100.

7. "Is the Notion," 75, 77, 100–101. Compare in this context Raimon Panikkar, *Myth, Faith and Hermeneutics* (New York: Paulist Press, 1979).

8. "Is the Notion," 90, 102. See also Raimon Panikkar, *The Cosmotheandric Experience: Emerging Religious Consciousness*, ed. Scott Eastham (Maryknoll, NY: Orbis Books, 1993). Regarding personhood, he adds ("Is the Notion," 91): "In drawing the distinction between individual and person I would put much more content in it than a French moral philosopher would do nowadays." The reference is apparently to Emmanuel Mounier, *Personalism*, trans. Philip Mairet (Notre Dame, IN: University of Notre Dame Press, 1970). To be sure, the notion of "personalism" is associated with numerous other thinkers, such as Max Scheler, Romano Guardini, and Karol Wojtyła (the later Pope John Paul II).

9. Compare Theodor W. Adorno, *Minima Moralia: Reflections from the Damaged Life*, trans. E. F. N. Jephcott (London: Verso, 1978).

10. See Henry Rosemont Jr., "Human Rights: A Bill of Worries," in *Confucianism and Human Rights*, ed. Wm. Theodore de Bary and Tu Weiming (New York: Columbia University Press, 1998), 57, 60.

11. Smitu Kothari and Harsh Sethi, eds., *Rethinking Human Rights* (Delhi: Lokayan, 1989), 9–11. See also Chandra Muzaffar, *Human Rights and the World Order* (Penang: Just World Trust, 1993), 39.

12. Kothari and Sethi, *Rethinking Human Rights*, 9.

13. See Panikkar, *Cosmotheandric Experience* (cited in note 8).

Chapter 9. Falling Upward Communally:
A Tribute to Richard Rohr

1. As previously indicated, this view had been advocated by the German (semi-fascist) Carl Schmitt who equated politics with warfare or the contest between friends and enemies. See Carl Schmitt, *The Concept of the Political* (1932), trans. George Schwab (Chicago: University of Chicago Press, 2007).

2. Richard Rohr, "A Journey to Freedom" and "True Liberation in God," meditation@ac.org, January 17 and 18, 2021. See also Allen Dwight Callahan, *The*

Talking Book: African Americans and the Bible (New Haven, CT: Yale University Press, 2006), 83; and Barbara A. Holmes, *Liberation and the Cosmos: Conversations with the Elders* (New York: Fortress Press, 2008). Compare also the comments of Vaclav Havel: "Liberation is an awareness of connections to a Reality beyond our reach, to a higher intention that is the source of all things, a higher authority to which we are all accountable in one way or another." See Vaclav Havel, *The Art of the Impossible: Politics as Morality in Practice* (New York: Knopf, 1997), 196.

3. See Richard Rohr, *The Universal Christ: How a Forgotten Reality Can Change Everything We See, Hope For, and Believe* (New York: Convergent Books, 2019). Philosophically, the issue of nondualism was first fully explored in Martin Heidegger, *Being and Time: A Translation of Sein und Zeit*, trans. John Macquarrie and Edward Robinson (San Francisco: Harper Collins, 1962).

4. Rohr, *Universal Christ*, 4–5, 7, 11. As he makes clear, nondualism of this kind is not just a doctrine but phenomenologically it is grounded in lived experience (7): "I don't want this to be a strictly 'theological' book if I can help it . . . Jesus did not come to earth so theologians alone could understand and make their mental distinctions, but so that 'they all may be one' (John 17:21)." He came to unite and to "reconcile all things in himself, everything in heaven and everything on earth (Colossians 1:19)."

5. *Universal Christ*, 14–15. Compare in this context my *Horizons of Difference: Engaging with Others* (Notre Dame, IN: University of Notre Dame Press, 2020), also my *Integral Pluralism: Beyond Culture Wars* (Lexington: University of Kentucky Press, 2010) and *Gemeinschaft und Differenz: Wege in die Zukunft* (Freiburg: Alber Verlag, 2018).

6. *Universal Christ*, 13, 15–16.

7. *Universal Christ*, 189–190, 194–197.

8. *Universal Christ*, 182, 194–197.

9. *Universal Christ*, 201.

10. See Karl Rahner, *The Trinity* (New York: Crossland, 1999), 10–11.

11. Richard Rohr (with Mike Morrell), *The Divine Dance: The Trinity and Your Transformation* (New Kensington, PA: Whitaker House, 2016), 27. The author cited is Elias Marechal, *Tears of the Innocent God* (New York: Paulist Press, 2015), 17.

12. Rohr, *Divine Dance*, 28–30.

13. *Divine Dance*, 36–37, 39.

14. Richard Rohr, *What Do We Do with Evil? The World, the Flesh, and the Devil* (Albuquerque: CAC, 2019), 1–2.

15. Richard Rohr, *Falling Upward: A Spirituality for the Two Halves of Life* (San Francisco: Jossey-Bass, 2012), vii–ix.

16. Rohr, *Falling Upward*, 73, 78, 85–86. See also Carl G. Jung, *The Collected Works*, vol. 1, *Psychiatric Studies* (Princeton, NJ: Princeton University Press, 1980), 480. The terms "true self" and "false self" are borrowed from Thomas Merton, *New Seeds of Contemplation* (New York: New Directions, 1962).

17. *Falling Upward*, 87–89, 91, 94.

18. *Falling Upward*, 153, 158–159.

19. *Falling Upward*, 162. See also Thomas Merton, *Collected Poems* (New York: New Direction, 1977), 279; also my "From Desert to Bloom: Thomas Merton's Contemplative Praxis," in my *Spiritual Guides: Pathfinders in the Desert* (Notre Dame, IN: University of Notre Dame, 2017), 57–75.

Concluding Remarks

1. Richard Rohr, *The Universal Christ* (New York: Convergent Books, 2019), 199–201.

2. Martin Luther King, Jr., *Where Do We Go from Here: Chaos or Community?* (Boston: Beacon Press, 1968), xvi, xx, 142, 201. King adds a passage from the First Letter of John (4:7, 12): "Let us love one another, for love is of God. If we love one another, God dwelleth in us, and his love is perfect in us."

3. June Jordan, "In Memoriam," in *Directed by Desire: The Collected Poems of June Jordan* (Port Townsend, WA: Copper Canyon Press, 2005), 6.

4. Amanda Gorman, *The Hill We Climb and Other Poems* (New York: Penguin Books, 2021).

INDEX

www.ingramcontent.com/pod-product-compliance
Lightning Source LLC
Chambersburg PA
CBHW030334270326
41926CB00010B/1625